drawing as a sacred activity

Spirit doesn't live up there in the clouds — it lives in your heart. Draw it into your everyday life with these simple, safe, effective, and very powerful drawing exercises.

Angel looking with unconditional love, Prismacolor pencil, 1990

drawing
as a sacred
activity

simple steps to explore your feelings
and heal your consciousness

heather c. williams

new world library
novato, california

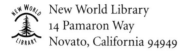

New World Library
14 Pamaron Way
Novato, California 94949

These drawing exercises are part of an experiential educational program based on humanistic, artistic, and spiritual principles that may or may not assist in personal growth. They are not intended to be psychotherapy or medical therapy or a substitute for either. Individuals may wish to share their drawings with their sponsor, counselor, therapist, healthcare provider, or minister, and this is wonderful.

The terminology (directions, extended directions, intersections, anchor points, constellations, collisions, and transitions) used in Section 1, Pencils & Perception, was first coined by Jan Valentin Saether. I learned this during my five-year apprenticeship with him. While Mr. Saether gives me permission to use this terminology, he wishes it to be known that he does not necessarily intend the same things or apply them to the same ends as I do.

Library of Congress Cataloging-in-Publication Data
Williams, Heather C.
  Drawing as a sacred activity : simple steps to explore your feelings and heal your consciousness / Heather C. Williams.
      p.   cm.
  ISBN 1-57731-224-4
  1. Drawing—Technique. 2. Personality and creative ability. I. Title.
  NC730 .W4925 2002
  741.2′01′9—dc21   2002007015

First Printing, September 2002
ISBN 1-57731-224-4
Printed in Canada on acid-free, partially recycled paper
Distributed to the trade by Publishers Group West

10 9 8 7 6 5 4 3 2

*This book is dedicated to every individual who yearns
to see her or his world in a new way.*

CONTENTS

Detail of drawing on page ii

Tree in backyard of the Milwaukee
house, ink, 1995

Student drawing (Sue), ink, 2000

Three birds and an Asian girl, ink, 2000

The real voyage of discovery consists not in seeking new landscapes but in having new eyes.

• • • Marcel Proust

PREFACE

I have always loved drawing, and I have always loved teaching and learning. After many years of using drawing to learn about my world and about myself, it seems completely natural that I give birth to a book about drawing. But this is not just a book about drawing. It is a book about the *sacred activity* of drawing. Almost everyone agrees that drawing can have a sacred quality. And almost everyone agrees that art (whether drawing, painting, sculpting, dancing, writing, singing, or playing an instrument) is a transformative process.

I was raised in the Lutheran Church and schooled in both public and parochial education. In sixth grade at St. Mark's Lutheran School, I drew a picture of the empty tomb at Easter viewed from the inside and looking out at a very amazed Mary Magdalene. Even as a child I was a contemplative sort of person. I wanted to experience the depth and the Spirit of life.

When I was twenty, my search began. I was searching for a Gurdjieff school when I left Wisconsin and came to San Francisco. Instead, I found Thane Walker. Although he did not have a Gurdjieff school, he had studied with Gurdjieff, and that was even better. My most formative years (between twenty and thirty-two) were spent taking classes in his school, the Prosperos School of Ontology. I was one of quite a number of young people who were searching. We were open to being shaped (if that is the right expression) by Thane's approach, which was to reach each student at his or her point of confusion and from there to guide the student toward his or her true identity as mind unfolding, as consciousness.

As consciousness, we can make positive changes. I have adopted this approach in my drawing classes and in this book. In it you will be asked to focus on the present moment, and from there you will be guided to draw out of yourself a new understanding.

When I was thirty-two, I returned to art and met Jan Valentin Saether, a Viking-like Norwegian master painter living in Venice, California. I was living nearby, and I began taking painting classes. Not long after that, he asked me (and two boys) to be his apprentices.

Circumstances forced Mr. Saether, his wife, Liv, their children, and two of the apprentices (one was me) to move to a large old house in Malibu. We boiled our own mediums and ground our own pigments. Painting class every Saturday began at 10 A.M. and ended at 5 P.M. Drawing class was every Tuesday evening, and on Friday evenings we had an open life-drawing workshop. I lived in Malibu for ten years. Because apprenticeship was not a paid position, I worked for the Malibu Temporary Agency during the day and painted at night and on weekends. Mr. Saether's tremendous influence on my life is visible in the first part of this book.

Life made another turn when Louise Hay came into my life. I found myself teaching art to people with AIDS both at the Hay Foundation and at Marianne Williamson's Hollywood Center for Living. There I met Lucia Capacchione, author of many books about drawing. Her work with the nondominant hand greatly influenced my own work. When Patricia Crane created the Louise Hay Teacher Training, with Ms. Hay's blessing, I was asked to be an associate teacher and present my drawing exercises at all the trainings. We trained more than eight hundred Louise Hay teachers from around the world over a period of six years. These teachers loved gaining access to their own inner wisdom through this new way of drawing. They motivated me to write part 2.

When I was forty-three years old, I moved back to Wisconsin for seven years. During this time of reconnecting with my family, I taught drawing at several universities as well as to inmates at the Milwaukee County Jail. Through ArtReach, a nonprofit organization in Milwaukee, I was hired to teach drawing to people living with manic depression, bulimia, developmental disabilities, and trauma; to teens in recovery from drugs and alcohol; to people living with schizophrenia, Alzheimer's disease, AIDS, and cancer; and to a group of homeless men living in a transitional housing project called the Open Gate. These people, some of whom were labeled as having severe disabilities, experienced profound insights through the drawing exercises — just like everyone else! They motivated me to write this book.

I illustrate *Drawing As a Sacred Activity* with more than 150 of my own drawings, reflecting nearly fifty years of seeing and more than 12,000 hours of life-drawing sessions. I am positively thrilled to bring my drawings out of my studio to share them with you. In addition, some of my students gave me permission to publish their drawings. I sincerely hope that you, my dear readers, will study our drawings and feel inspired to explore drawing as a sacred activity yourself.

If you are just starting to draw, or if you are getting back to it after several years, please be gentle with yourself. Instead of comparing your work with other people's, put your energy into listening and following the directions that you see in nature. Your point of view is one of your most sacred possessions. No one but you has your unique perspective. As you embark on your drawing journey, you will encounter bumps and potholes, and sometimes the going may get pretty rough. When you feel drawn to using the exercises in this book, especially if you are in pain or confused, give yourself a lot of space to experiment, explore, make mistakes, and feel foolish. Let your heart guide your hand to the great awakening — your true identity as mind unfolding.

The
birds
fly
to
Remind
me
to
lift
My
eyes
and
My
thoughts.

My beloved inner friend, ink, 2000

My own Eternal Self
Live Thou Thy life in me.
Do Thou Thy will in me.
Be Thou made flesh in me.
I have no will but Thine.
I have no Self but Thee.
*And so it is.**

The Naskapi Indians of the forests of the Labrador Peninsula live in solitude with no tribal customs or religious teachers to tell them what to believe. To the Naskapi, our soul is simply an inner companion (or "friend"). The major obligation of the Naskapis is to follow the instructions given by their dreams and then to give permanent form to their contents in art. Lies and dishonesty drive the inner companion away, while generosity toward and love of one's neighbors and of animals attract this companion and give it life.

• • • M. L. von Franz
from *Man and His Symbols,*
edited by Carl G. Jung

---

* Adapted from "Transcendental Meditation", The Prosperos.

INTRODUCTION

the benefits of drawing

The activity of drawing is natural to every human being — just watch any child left alone with paper and crayon. We all have an inborn need to connect our inner and outer world in a meaningful way — and drawing is a satisfactory and powerful way to do just that. It is also a safe way to see old, familiar things in a new light. How often do you sit quietly for a few moments, calm down, relax, and reconnect with a deeper aspect of yourself? It is well known that drawing develops greater hand-eye coordination, enhances your ability to see what is in front of you, and improves your capacity to think visually (very helpful in developing creative ideas).

In my desire to help others experience the many benefits of drawing, I wrote the book you now hold in your hands. I have divided this book into three distinct parts, each of which begins with an introductory discussion and leads toward a group of drawing exercises. In part 1, "Pencils and Perception," you will focus outward on the physical world of people, places, and objects. Normally by the time you are a grown adult you are conditioned to believe that people, places, and things are separate from you. You can name everything you see: That's a tree, a table, a lamp, a man. Naming what you see is different from drawing what you see. Drawing exercises a different part of your brain. Whereas naming something sets you apart from what you see, drawing connects you to it. When you feel connected to

In the twenty-first century, we may fulfill what the first half of the twentieth century foreshadowed — that seeing must not be limited to evidence alone, because the evidence is shaped by the seeing that beholds it.

••• Philip Golabuk,
Science of Mind interview, March 2000

3

Head of young man, ink, 1995

I make a head to see how I see, to know how I see — not to make a work of art.

• • • Alberto Giacometti

something, you are more likely to take care of it — even to have compassion for it. Each exercise in part 1 provides a specific focus for you to work with. I have also included warm-up exercises to help you draw what you see in the world around you. Even if you like imaginative drawings, fantasy creations, or abstract works, I'm sure you will find these warm-up exercises beneficial.

Part 2, "Crayons and Consciousness," will help you focus inward on the interior landscape of memories, emotions, dreams, unconscious patterns, and your heart's wisdom. The unconscious mind is a vast, new territory awaiting your exploration. Psychology is a relatively new science, only about one hundred years old. And while therapists and counselors can help you sort things out, they cannot go with you into your memories. They cannot feel your feelings. They cannot give up an old attitude and replace it with a new understanding. *You* are the only one who can do these things. Drawing is a safe, effective, relevant, and playful way to explore your inner world. The exercises in part 2 provide clear directions for you to follow as you explore your emotional feelings and draw them out of you. If at any time you feel that you could use professional help in processing some of the emotions that come up during these exercises, call your counselor, minister, or therapist. And take the drawing with you!

You will focus inward again in part 3, only this time you will be focusing on a more subtle aspect of the unconscious mind — your intuitive feelings. Another name for intuition is the still, small voice inside you. Everyone has this voice; however, not everyone listens to it. The two exercises in this section are designed to help you cross the threshold in consciousness so that you can listen to and feel the intuitive wisdom within you.

Drawing Helps You To

1. Connect with the world before you in a meaningful and heartfelt way.
2. Open up to a whole new world that is right before your eyes but that you don't see because you are thinking of other things.
3. Feel safe and secure in the world.
4. Calm down, relax, and find peace.
5. Develop the skill of seeing.
6. Develop greater hand-eye coordination.
7. Explore the right side of your brain.

perception: three aspects

Everything starts with perception — how we see things. Although it's central to our daily experience, we seldom think about our perception and its influence on our lives. Perception consists of three aspects: sensory, psychological/neurological, and intuitive. The five senses form the sensory aspect of perception — seeing, smelling, touching, hearing, and tasting. You perceive this book (and everything else) by seeing it with your eyes. Look up from this book and notice what your senses are reporting to you.

You also have responses, reactions, feelings, and judgments about what you see with your

The more you look at something, the more you find.

• • • Kay Andrews, proofreader

Copy of Edward Burne-Jones, ink, 1995

eyes (or what you taste, touch, hear, and smell). You interpret things differently from how your neighbor, sister, partner, and children do, because your interpretations are based on your mental and emotional constructs. You compare this with that, form a conclusion about it, and name the thing you see — based on your interpretation or present understanding. The psychological and neurological aspect of perception allows you to label events, situations, people. You form beliefs. Sometimes the labels and beliefs are accurate, and sometimes they are not. It can be shocking when our perception does not conform to reality and we are forced to change. But this change moves us forward, and that is good.

The intuitive aspect of perception allows us to perceive something immediately — without actually seeing, hearing, smelling, tasting, or touching it and without intellectually figuring anything out. We know something in our hearts — this is intuitive perception. Everyone has this capacity. Drawing is a safe, playful way to explore all three aspects of your perception.

I want to add a brief word about the difference between *perception* and *conception*. Perception involves feelings. It is recognition and interpretation of sensory stimuli (based chiefly on memory). It is also insight, intuition, or knowledge gained by perceiving. Conception is the ability to form or understand mental beliefs and abstractions. Concepts are conceived in the mind; they are plans, ideas, and thoughts. Concepts and percepts work together. You think about something, and

Humphreys Hotel, ink, 1997

suddenly you have a feeling about it. Or you experience a feeling about something and mentally form a belief about it. Many people think, think, think consciously and feel, feel, feel unconsciously. This book offers you a playful way to become more conscious of feeling.

three different ways to draw out your feelings

Feelings are the core of every relationship and the foundation of the arts. Yet as primary as they are, feelings are shunned, denied, avoided, and greatly misunderstood in our civilization. We are frightened of our feelings. And there are still few classes teaching you how to express them. Although we are all too aware of epidemic problems like drive-by shootings, domestic violence, child abuse, and so on, society as a whole does not make the connection between repressed feelings and violence, and these feelings are denied every day.

Boy at middle school, ink, 2000

No one but you can look through your eyes, think your thoughts, or feel your feelings. No one but you can draw out your feelings — be they painful and conflicted or positive and sublime. Drawing is one way to *feel your feelings.* I think of drawing as a dialogue between you and your feelings. Drawing is a safe and healthy way to become aware of your feelings, to listen to your heart, to explore your thinking, to make changes, and to breathe fresh air, emotionally speaking. The feelings in your heart are prompting you to change; drawing is a safe, effective, and playful way to listen.

love is essential

We all have talents, abilities, and proclivities toward certain ways of expressing and revealing ourselves to our families, communities, and the world at large. One person likes to dance, another prefers reading, another acting and singing. Many people (who stopped drawing around the age of nine) feel convinced that they have no talent or ability for drawing. I hear this all the time. "I have no talent — I draw stick figures!" This kind of statement is usually shouted at me with a kind of bravado, but I sense pain underneath it. Remember, there is nothing wrong with stick figures.

Unrealistic expectations paralyze people creatively. Use the drawing exercises in this book as a journey into your own perceptions, of your experience of seeing through your eyes. In no way am I promoting my own style of drawing. I am not suggesting that your drawing goal ought to be to produce drawings that resemble the work of Rembrandt or of any other recognized artist. My challenge to you, dear readers — to take up your pen or pencil and love your world by seeing it firsthand — is rooted in the assumption that you can do significant things with your eyes, hands, and heart. Furthermore, your family, friends, and community are dependent on some of its members doing just that. You already have within you what it takes to do this. Drawing is one way to bring it out.

If you have ever watched children, you must agree that all of us are born with an ability to express feelings. It is natural for children to put their feelings on paper. It is natural for children to draw their mommy and daddy, to draw their perception of these people and things in the world. Society's fads and fashions come and go. Styles in art become popular, then fade away. What remains are the marks drawn by people who love deeply and follow their hearts.

Drawing, dancing, singing, acting, playing the piano, painting, sculpting — all forms of art draw on the one sacred Source for their power. Neither the oil industry nor the big-money movie industry contains the power that artists channel into their work. The power of art is interior, and it becomes available to you when you begin turning within and drawing it out of you. It is an unfolding process. It does not happen overnight.

Milwaukee life-drawing workshop,
Prismacolor pencil, 1996

Pencils and Perception: Drawing Objective Feelings

When you think of drawing you probably think of an artist using a pencil to draw a still life, portrait, or landscape.

To draw what you see, you need to feel connected to it and to trust your eyes. Feeling connected is natural. The drawing exercises in this part of the book focus on the outer world. They give you a basic key so that you can draw what you see — regardless of your talent or proclivity for drawing.

Crayons and Consciousness: Drawing Emotional Feelings

Everyone must learn to express emotional feelings safely. Society tells us to stuff

Milwaukee life-drawing workshop,
Prismacolor pencil, 1996

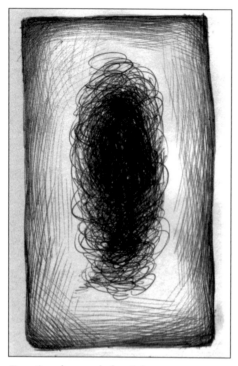

Emotional overwhelm, ink, 1997

Boy contemplating an intuitive thought, ink, 2000

our feelings and say we are fine. As a result many people are walking around overwhelmed and ready to explode. Drawing is a perfect way to let out these unexpressed feelings. When you draw out your emotional feelings, you don't worry about proportions. You simply focus your attention, feel your feelings, and express on paper what is in your heart. Although it may seem simple, drawing is a very powerful way to let your feelings flow.

Crayons are colorful and childlike, perfect for expressing the sometimes dark shadow part of you as well as the vibrant and magnificent part of you. Drawing is a great way to take in a deep refreshing breath of air, emotionally speaking, and to let it go.

Ink and Intuition: Drawing Intuitive Feelings

Intuitive feelings are understood through a balanced and centered mind, so some kind of meditative preparation is necessary before drawing these kinds of feelings out. Intellectual striving to control the pencil is put on the back burner of your mind when doing this kind of drawing. On the front burner is a deep openness and a willingness to let go of knowing what is going to happen on your paper. This is also not the place for emotional venting.

Intuitive insights come out of the blue. You have to be willing to be surprised. Not filtered through the intellect or persuaded by the emotions, these subtle feelings are like wise advisors. When you quiet down and learn to listen, they unconditionally love you and guide you through life's many changes. Being both alert and relaxed is important.

learning differences and visual thinking

I can't read. I can't focus. I can't write.

There have always been kids who had trouble adjusting to the written page, to homework and the routine of school. However, today there are millions of these kids. Dyslexia, ADD (attention deficit disorder), ADHD (attention deficit hyperactive disorder): All these syndromes were unheard of when I was growing up. As a child, I had long stretches of quiet and plenty of space. I could ponder life, organize my thoughts and feelings, and integrate what I saw and heard, allowing me to make sense out of things.

Today things are different. There is little time to ponder life. We turn the computer, television, or radio on first thing in the morning. We drive to work listening to news or music. We have email waiting to be read. Our cell phones are ringing. A blizzard of information swirls around us. Problems from around the world cry out to be understood and solved.

"We live in an age of parenthesis," said John Naisbett, author of *Megatrends*. "The values that gave meaning to our parents and hundreds of thousands of ancestors before them no longer hold meaning. We feel anchorless and adrift." Long ago, everyone in indigenous cultures drew, painted, sculpted, sang, chanted, and danced to connect with the ancestors, the environment, one another, and to Spirit. They

In the years ahead, I believe that perceptual skills combined with verbal skills will be viewed as the basic necessities for creative human thought. Learning to see and draw is a very efficient way to train the visual system, just as learning to read can efficiently train the verbal system.

••• Betty Edwards,
Drawing on the Artist Within

Teenager sitting down, ink, 2001

Every problem I've ever solved started with my ability to visualize and see the world in pictures.

••• Temple Grandin,
Thinking in Pictures and Other Reports from My Life with Autism

I think best in pictures.

••• Don Winkler, severely dyslexic CEO

were not so obsessed with working, making money, buying things, and looking good. Long ago everyone was an artist. There was no art market to put a price on creativity. There were no critics to compare you with others. There was only the celebration. You showed up and you did your best.

This book began three years ago with a little ten-page booklet that I prepared for a drawing workshop in England and Italy. At that time my drawings stimulated my thoughts. How easily that little booklet was created.

Then a desire to write a real book began to grow in me. But although drawings express deep, rich textural thoughts and feelings, the words took me far away from my drawings and my feelings. Many times I woke up to realize that I had written myself into a philosophical corner and a creative dead-end. I had to backtrack, erase, delete, and finally stop in frustration. What in the world was going on? Was it this hard for everyone who writes? Drawing is my favorite subject — so why was it so difficult to express my ideas about it?

In desperation I called my friend Analise Rigan, a wonderful artist. She had written a book years ago. She asked me, Have you tried the storyboard method of writing? A storyboard is a visual layout of a book, movie, or whatever you are creating. I went to my friend's house, looked at her storyboard, and ran home and created a visual layout for my book. It now flowed quite well. Of course, there was still lots and lots of work to do, but it became clear to me that my thinking flows from a visual orientation.

The first advantage of thinking in pictures was that it was apparently much quicker. The second advantage was that the statements in pictures were much more comprehensive.

• • • Joanna Field,
On Not Being Able to Paint

Teenager standing up, ink, 2001

I wonder about kids labeled "learning disabled." Is their thinking basically all right — just oriented more toward the visual kind of thinking rather than verbal thinking? Could learning how to draw open the door for these kids to think verbally? This is new territory, and you are invited to explore it with me. Draw first, then write about the drawing. Do words flow easier for you once you have drawn? What discoveries do you make?

left and right: two ways of seeing and thinking

The subject of drawing always seems to bring up a discussion of the two distinct hemispheres of the brain, which fortunately are joined together and work as a team processing information in different ways.

The left hemisphere processes information logically and sequentially. Highly verbal and intellectual, it likes to measure, compare, analyze, and make decisions. The left side of the brain is comfortable knowing the names of things. It is good at planning trips, figuring out what makes the clock tick, balancing the checkbook, and estimating the time it takes to run a mile. It is competitive.

In contrast, the right hemisphere is cooperative. It processes information spatially, holistically, and visually. This means it sees several aspects at once, thinks about the whole, and notices connections, be they physical, emotional, or intuitive. Highly relational, the right brain likes to imagine, draw, drive on the freeway, arrange the furniture in a room,

If you want to be creative, stay in part a child with the creativity and invention that characterizes children before they are deformed by adult society.

• • • Jean Piaget

Adam and Eve, ink, 2000

13

and sense the emotional temperature of people on the street.

Many books have already been written on the subject of the left and right hemispheres of the brain, though more research is clearly needed. We in the West are strongly conditioned to look at things almost exclusively with our left brains, that is, logically. We praise our children when they name things. We assess school children with standardized tests. (Talk about left brain!) We compare, analyze, and judge just about everything: We even look at ourselves as objects and judge ourselves as such.

How does this discussion relate to drawing? To draw we have to shift gears from left to right. Instead of looking at things and people as objects existing in space and time, isolated and separate, we have to look for relationships. You see a tree before you. In your ordinary state of mind you see the tree as a separate thing. Activate your artist's eye, and although at first you will see the tree as a separate thing, you will look for things that connect visually with it. Fences, buildings, telephone wires, rocks, distant hills, even people may be standing nearby, and from your point of view, they intersect with the tree. The artist's eye in you is excited to see things intersect, connect, and relate. Looking at things in a new way is a very healthy activity.

Medical autopsies have shown evidence of healthy, pink, flexible brain cells in old people who have exercised their minds (changed their minds) often throughout their lives. Compare this with hard, inflexible brain cells found in old people who did not have a history of

Detail of drawing on page 17

changing their minds. They liked to think the same old thoughts day in, day out. Resistance to changing your mind may not serve you well in your later years. Go with the flow, stretch yourself, open your heart, and change your mind once in a while. This practice is a healthy way to stay vigorous and youthful.

When you are drawing and you discover that the lines on your paper are tight and rigid, you do not need to rip up the drawing in frustration and declare to the world that you just can't draw! Simply realize that your left brain is a bit too dominant. All you need to do is open up a bit. Think relationships. Notice vertical, horizontal, and diagonal directions and feel connected with the way they relate to one another. Look carefully at the curved surfaces where transitions between light and dark are soft and gradual. The warm-up exercises in part 1 will teach you how to do this.

Here is a little exercise you can do to practice seeing with your right brain. You can do it while standing in line at the grocery store, bank, or anywhere. First, become aware when you are judging people. You can tell when you are judging; your eyes and tummy get tight and rigid. Second, shift into your drawing eye, your right brain. Notice how your tummy and eyes immediately soften. Look at one person and notice her eyebrows. Are they horizontal? Diagonal? Look at the vertical line of her neck where it intersects with her shoulder. Feel the slope of it. What is behind her that intersects with her shoulder — shelves, trees, buildings, other people?

Suddenly you are looking at things differently. You are looking with your artist's eye!

Through our perception of the objective qualities of the sense world we awaken to the activity of spirit within the world of matter.

• • • Rudolf Steiner,
Art As Spiritual Activity

Images tend to travel deeper than words into the unconscious.

• • • Gregg M. Furth,
The Secret World of Drawings

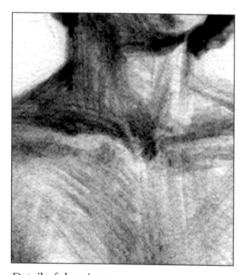

Detail of drawing on page 17

the balancing act

When I look with my artist's eye, I feel good. Judgments dissolve. Memories and criticisms fade. My heart opens to the present moment, and new possibilities pop into my mind. Try this and see for yourself. Feel your energy shift, become softer, more sensual, more relaxed, open, and juicy. It is easy to shift your consciousness from left brain (separate, decisive, judgmental, firm) to right (relational, open, and soft), and back again, if necessary.

Is right good and left bad? No. You want to use the attributes of both sides of your brain. We've talked about what happens when you are out of balance and relying too much on the logical part of you. What about when you rely too much on the relational part of you?

When your right brain becomes too dominant, your drawing (and your life) takes on a vague aimless look. It feels kind of bland and blah. What can you do? The remedy is to make a few decisions somewhere on the paper (or in your life). Make strong decisions of dark and light. Reclarify the directions. Establish boundaries.

Drawings (and life) are exciting when right and left brain work together, back and forth creating depth and movement on paper and in life. The artist's way of seeing life is playful. Imagine a seesaw. Picture two children sitting on this seesaw. The left brain sits on one end, and the right on the other. Up goes left brain (seeing objects, pieces, and parts, making decisions and boundaries). Down goes right brain. Then, right brain goes up (seeing relationships, intersections, connections). Then down goes left brain, and so on.

While the ups and downs of life can be fun, they can also be exasperating. Thankfully, there is more to life than going up and down. The seesaw illustrates a *third* way of seeing. Every seesaw has a center called the fulcrum (or hinge or lever). This center stays in place while the two ends go up and down. *Fulcrum* is defined as "an agent through which vital powers are exercised." This centered part of life is constant and does not change, does not go up and down or back and forth.

Here is the empowering aspect of art: When you stand at the center of yourself and express your heart and soul in whatever form of art you love, you become a channel through which the vital power of life flows. Sing! Dance! Draw! Paint! What a powerful being you are!

Being centered is powerful and invaluable. You can be centered within yourself anywhere and at any time — in jail, in a terrible storm, in the midst of a divorce, in a new job, when you feel creatively blocked.

No one can make you be centered — because you already are. Accept all of yourself. Some situations call for more contrast of dark and light, hardness, clarity, and decisiveness. Some situations call for more relatedness, softness, and appreciation of the gray areas of life. You have a choice in how you respond to life.

Creativity is a balancing act, moment by moment. The constant center of you is always accessible within your heart. In the center of your brain is the center of balance that helps you

Form always points back to an ordering principle.

• • • Rudolf Steiner,
Art As Spiritual Activity

Malibu life-drawing workshop,
Prismacolor pencil, 1985

Our deepest fear is not that we are inadequate. Our deepest fear is that we are powerful beyond measure. It is our light, not our darkness, that frightens us. We ask ourselves, Who am I to be brilliant, gorgeous, talented, and fabulous? Actually, who are you not to be?

• • • Marianne Williamson

Milwaukee life-drawing workshop, Prismacolor pencil, 1993

stand up and walk. In the center of your heart is another center of balance that helps you to make changes, to feel connected to the outer world, and to make decisions and set boundaries.

mistakes and accidents: another view

A hardened heart and rigid, narrow thinking form the greatest danger to the creative part of your mind. Add arrogance, and you really are over the edge. Someone who knows it all, whose mind is made up, who has an agenda and no interest in listening to other viewpoints is not able to contribute to the moment creatively. Inflexible, brittle, and rigid, they are stuck in their left brains. It does no good to point fingers. We have all been there and done that. It is an ongoing encounter.

As an artist, what can you do to break free of such rigidity? The artist Francis Bacon once said that the key ingredient to his painting success was his willingness to consciously and deliberately create accidents on his canvas. What? Why would anyone want to create accidents? Because accidents open up your mind and heart to new ideas and to new possibilities, and that's creative.

Initially you panic when you make a wrong mark on the paper. You think, "Oh, no, I've ruined it!" Instead of ripping up your drawing, make something out of it. While drawing, I make all kinds of odd, extra lines as I try to find the neck, mouth, shoulder, leg. Mistakes can make the drawing richer, more alive and exciting than a technically perfect line drawing.

Why not experiment with accidents on paper or canvas? No one gets hurt, and your brain cells get some exercise. Besides, you will discover that looking for possibilities feels good. Start with something simple — draw a line. Make a mistake. Now make something out of it. It's stimulating and fun!

interpreting your drawings lightheartedly

Everything you do, see, and hear you interpret through your present state of consciousness. We interpret everything. Sometimes our interpretations are judgmental and moralistic. We say, "This is good!" or "This is bad!" "This is ugly" or "This is lovely." We need to be careful when we interpret our drawings and other creative works, especially while we are still in the process of learning.

What does a drawing mean? Therapists and analytical people love to interpret emotions, drawings, behaviors. I get into this myself sometimes. But we have to be careful. When it comes to drawing, adults are not much different from children. Suzanne Dixon, professor emeritus of pediatrics at the University of California at San Diego, says, "What children choose to draw and how they draw reflects how they think about their world."

Drawing can help you gain insights into your thoughts and feelings. Be gentle with yourself as you draw, no matter how long you have been doing it. If you are just beginning, be extra gentle, kind, and considerate. Praise yourself for showing up to practice.

If ordinary people really knew that consciousness and not matter is the link that connects us with each other and the world, then their views about war and peace, environmental pollution, social justice, religious values, and all other human endeavors would change radically.

•••Amit Goswami,
The Self-Aware Universe

Yearning to express, ink, 1995

One of my teachers in Australia wrote me saying that some of her students draw slowly using lots of lines and colors, while others finish quickly and then feel disappointed — as if they didn't get as much out of the experience as the others. What could she do to help them? I told her that her job was to be unconditionally supportive of all her students, whether they drew quickly or slowly. Everyone is here to learn. Each person has something different to learn. There is no right way to draw. There is no wrong way to draw.

Perhaps those who finish quickly and are disappointed in themselves approach other areas of their lives in the same way. Drawing will allow them to see this pattern and to choose to make a change, if they wish to. Perhaps those who finish slowly wish they could be faster.

Paper and bits of graphite, ink, or crayon are tangible residues of a mental and emotional experience. A mind makes these marks. A mind interprets these marks. Be lighthearted and childlike. Be willing to let your mind and heart unfold. Be willing to explore and play with new patterns.

how to use this book

I invite you to dip into this book wherever you need to focus in the moment. There is no right or wrong way. Follow your heart — it is your most important teacher. Work exclusively in one part, or read all three. If you find yourself with some time on your hands (waiting for your child at school or for the plane to depart), turn to part 1 and explore the world around you in a new way. Follow the pathway of visual directions that you see before you. Notice new patterns and become aware of what you didn't see before. If you find yourself creatively blocked or in a moment of emotional upheaval, turn to part 2 and draw on your own inner wisdom to guide you to a new understanding. Accept your emotions. Use them to gain access to your inner wisdom and to see new aspects of your situation. If you are in the midst of a life-changing experience or at a turning point and you feel that you are facing an unknown future, turn to part 3 and practice a creative way to cross the threshold and accept the gift of the transformation that is upon you. Follow your hunches. Trust that something greater than yourself is guiding your hand, your steps in the present situation, and your heart as you listen to your intuition.

At the back of the book you will find a suggested reading list of books about drawing, visual thinking, spirituality, healing, and other topics. I invite you to use these sources to learn more about drawing, about yourself, about your sacred place in the world. I have also included an alphabetical index of all the exercises in the book.

Happy drawing!

pencils and perception

exploring your feelings toward
objects, nature, and people

Objective feeling, boy on front page of the *Los Angeles Times* the day Mother Teresa died, graphite, 1998

Drawing is the discipline by which I constantly rediscover the world.

• • • Frederick Franck, *The Zen of Seeing*

INTRODUCTION

the adventure of seeing

Every day in every city on the planet people in drawing classes gather around arrangements of flowers, drapery, or a live person — and draw! They spend hours exploring the adventure of seeing and drawing.

Drawing accelerates and quickens a kind of seeing that allows you access to a part of your mind that is different from the part you are accustomed to using. It involves a different kind of thinking. Any time that you exercise your mind in this way, you see something new. And this experience is very refreshing, even liberating. It can also be very challenging to the way you have come to think of things.

No machine or technological wizardry can get inside your head, look out at the world through your eyes, and describe what you see. This seeing business is very personal, which is why I say that drawing is an individual adventure of seeing. Only you stand inside your thoughts, behind your eyes, aware of what you are seeing, feeling, and thinking. Only you can go where no one has gone before — on an inner journey to explore and see the world as it is — as energy, as consciousness.

When you first begin drawing, you are challenged by the limits and distortions of your ordinary left-brain way of seeing. This is the scary and irritating side of drawing. I've seen many people hit the wall, so to speak, when they come up against the fact that their ordinary way of seeing just does not facilitate

Perceiving accomplishes at the sensory level what in the realm of reasoning is known as understanding. Eyesight is insight.

••• Rudolf Arnheim,
Art and Visual Perception

Detail of drawing on page 17

*People should learn to see
and so avoid all danger.*

• • • Buddha

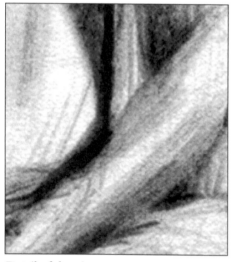

Detail of drawing on page 17

drawing. Even artists who have been drawing for years have to shift their thinking to draw what they see.

It is good to know that other ways of seeing are available to you. There are parts of your brain that easily embrace visual information. When you know what to look for, you can draw what you see.

Lawrence Wechsler wrote a book called *Seeing Is Forgetting the Name of the Thing One Sees* about the life of Los Angeles artist Robert Irwin. In it he quotes Irwin as saying, "Physicalness is experienced perceptually." In other words, forget the names of the things you are looking at when you want to draw or paint them. Instead, look for perceptual relationships. This concept is the basis of my drawing classes.

In this part of the book you will learn how to see. By practicing the basic directions in the warm-ups and by doing the drawing exercises, you will find yourself very naturally drawing a felt sense of what you are looking at. Your drawings will express your natural style, which, fortunately, is already within you. You do not have to invent it or create it out of thin air. It can be drawn out of you with practice, patience, willingness, and lots of love.

This kind of perceptual drawing may initially stretch your mind, but once you get into the flow of it, it will become much easier, and it will also become therapeutic. You will have to open your heart to yourself while you are learning. You will have to let love be your goal rather than academic standards, your mother's approval, gallery sales, or just plain old self-imposed notions of perfection. Your heart sees things as a child does — very simply. This kind of looking and drawing opens your heart so that you can see the world as it is. It is far more beautiful than you can imagine.

Remember, no matter how old you are or how young, no matter how knowledgeable you are about art and drawing or how ignorant you are about such things — your point of view is very important. Your point of view is all you are working with — no matter what you are looking at.

trusting your eyes

Although trusting your eyes is simple, it can be challenging at first. Even after years of drawing, I still have to consciously remind myself to relax and simply look for vertical, horizontal, and diagonal directions, intersections, and relationships.

Just the other day I had a few minutes after church to sit in the outdoor patio and draw. A chair caught my eye, and I began to draw it. Pretty quickly I realized how rigid my drawing was and how limited and serious I felt trying to get this chair on my paper. When you find yourself drawing this way, stop! It's too confining, limiting, difficult, and serious to draw just the chair. Back up and look for lines that intersect it — the table in front of it, the plants and the tree behind it.

In other words, look for relationships. Ah. I began to let the drawing unfold through me. I relaxed and fell into the part of me that is interested in seeing lines, directions, and relationships.

Detail of drawing on page 17

It is only through a sense of the right relation of things that freedom can be obtained.

• • • Robert Henri, *The Art Spirit*

Detail of drawing on page 17

The real study of an art student is more a development of that sensitive nature and appreciative imagination with which he was so fully endowed when a child, and which, unfortunately in almost all cases, the contact with the grown-ups shames out of him before he has passed into what is understood as real life.

• • • Robert Henri, *The Art Spirit*

Instead of drawing things, draw the field in which the things exist. The field includes both the object that attracts your eye and the objects that surround and interact with it. Draw a direction of the arm and a direction that intersects it. Believe it or not, this makes drawing far easier and much more exciting. You are just using a different way of seeing.

Drawing the field instead of just the object helps you to focus in a soft and lighthearted way. Chairs, trees, lamps, even people can be thought of as hard, substantial, and serious objects, yet when you approach them in this new way — as a field of relationships — they soften. And *you* soften. Lift yourself out of your ordinary judgmental way of seeing things and focus on what is before your eyes. Be playful. You will see how powerful and simple it can be when you trust your eyes and your heart.

Frederick Franck says in his book *The Zen of Seeing,* "Don't 'think' about what you are drawing, just let the hand follow what the eye sees."

In other words, the rules for drawing begin with trust. Trust your eyes. Trust your hands. Trust your heart. And lighten up! Perfection is not the goal. Academic standards, gallery standards, parental standards, and university standards are not important here. Meaningful connection is the goal.

In mathematics there is one right answer. But in drawing there are many right answers. Mathematics primarily exercises the left hemisphere of the brain, while drawing primarily exercises the right. Electricity needs both positive and negative. So do we. It just so happens that the right hemisphere is kind of like an orphan in the world. Few people claim it, nurture it, care for its expression.

Gertrude Stein asked Henri Matisse whether, when eating a tomato, he looked at it the way an artist would. Matisse replied: "No, when I eat a tomato I look at it the way anyone else would. But when I paint a tomato, then I see it differently."

A student who had never drawn before said to me after reading my manuscript and practicing on her own: "I can make sense of the outside world when I see in this way. I feel safer in the world."

"The activity of art is the activity of transformation," says Jan Valentin Saether, the master narrative painter and Gnostic priest with whom I apprenticed for five years in Malibu, California. The real power of art is that it provides each person who practices it with a basis of internal trust for dealing with the world. You do not change anything out there; you change your view, and then the world changes.

why feeling is so important

Feeling is important in drawing because it brings you into the present moment with all the particulars that exist in that moment. Hands, eyes, thoughts, and feelings all work together as one, connecting you with your world.

You have ideas about trees and people. Ideas are general perceptions. Most of the time we see quick versions of trees and people —

When we practice not making assumptions, we learn to see objectively — we don't justify anything, we don't judge or condemn, we don't take positions for or against, we don't lie to ourselves to protect our self-image. We simply see things as they are. Looking at things objectively and nonjudgmentally opens up a pathway out of the dream of hell.

• • • Don Miguel Ruiz,
from *Science of Mind,* February 1999

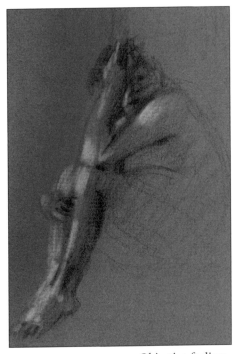

Objective feeling,
prismacolor pencil, 1988

just enough to steer clear of them when we are walking or driving.

A young boy points to his father and says, "Daddy." He doesn't say that about every man. When you slow down, focus, and draw a particular tree or a particular person, then your feelings enter into that picture. There is no doubt that your feelings affect your objectivity and perception. Drawing your objective feelings is a positive way to relate to your world.

When you draw, you become a channel, a midwife, a vehicle, if you will, expressing things in life that are real yet they are not completely or fully present until you see them. This section of the book guides you to become more aware of your unique view of the world. No one looks through your eyes but you! With awareness you can make changes, see things more clearly, see what is really there.

You can see the grace and weight of a tree or person. You can see that it has a place in the world. You also notice other things, like the bumps and knobby places on the tree's bark, the way it thrusts up out of the ground. You notice the pain in the man's eyes and the tilt of his head.

Drawing helps you open your heart and develop a deep, loving, and lasting relationship with what you are looking at. This relationship, like all relationships, asks something of you. It asks that you accept it as it is.

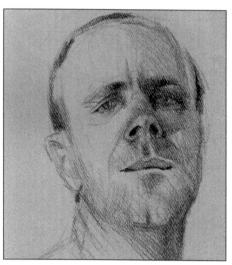

Objective feeling, Milwaukee life-drawing workshop, Prismacolor pencil, 1997

looking with soft eyes

When you look with soft eyes, you can connect with what you are looking at. Seeing with soft eyes enables you to imagine you are feeling the edges, the coolness or warmth, the pressure and weight of the form — whatever it is. Every form has edges you can see. Relax and feel and allow, rather than intellectually labeling the object and then trying to force that label to magically appear on the paper.

A deep connection takes time.

What is most important to you right now? Whatever it is, do it. It might be to close this book and catch a plane or return to the papers on your desk. It might be that right now is a good time to sit quietly and really look at your world. You will be amazed at how rich your life really is when you stop for a few minutes and just be with what is around you.

When you consciously draw something that you are being with, the moment is eternalized in you, and every time you look at that drawing you remember that moment. A drawing allows you to share these special moments with your friends and family. This is often a much deeper level of sharing than just chatting and hanging out.

My kind of drawing is a deepening down to the belly of your life, to the very soul of your existence. It is a journey. It is an unfolding process. Your awareness is unfolding. Your sense of yourself is unfolding. Your beliefs about the world are unfolding. You are learning to be with yourself as you unfold and grow and change and expand. Truth is the part of you that is changeless. The kind of drawing you will learn about in this book helps you begin to be aware of this deeper part of yourself.

The essence of drawing is that every mark on the paper should be one's own, growing out of the uniqueness of one's own psycho-physical structure and experience, not a mechanical copy of the model, however skillful.

• • • Joanna Field,
On Not Being Able to Paint

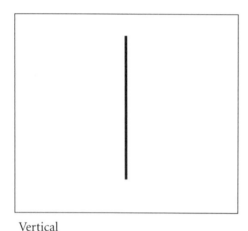

Vertical

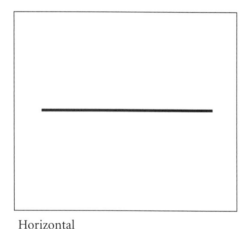

Horizontal

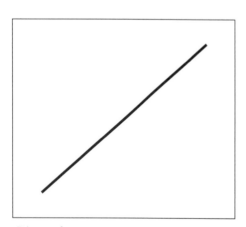

Diagonal

Warm-Up Exercises

basic directions: vertical, horizontal, diagonal

The world before your eyes may be so full of information that you become overwhelmed and do not know where to begin to draw. You must find a way to begin that makes sense to you. My students love the simplicity of directions. When they sit down to draw, they relax, soften their eyes, and look for one direction that feels accessible to them. From there they move on, looking for the next direction.

What do I mean by a direction? A direction is a vertical, horizontal, or diagonal edge of something, seen from your particular point of view. Objects (doors, trees, faces, fences) exist in space and time, while a direction or edge exists only in your point of view. For example, stand directly before a closed door. Notice that the top of the door appears to be horizontal. Open the door and notice that the top now appears to be diagonal. The door is still a door, physically and conceptually. But perceptually speaking, the direction changes, because the door has moved and is now at a different angle. You can only draw your point of view. You get in trouble on your paper when you try to draw the *concept* of door.

Place your finger on each line pictured here and trace the direction. Check them out for yourself. To me, vertical feels strong, spirited, independent, and quite different from horizontal. Horizontal feels peaceful, flat, restful.

It feels different from diagonal. Diagonal feels odd, intriguing, mysterious, quirky.

On paper, each of these three directions serves a unique purpose. Each conveys unique attributes or characteristics. Each of these three directions is accessible, easy to see, and as easy to draw for beginners as they are for advanced artists.

vertical directions and attributes

No matter where you choose to look, you will find vertical directions: in tree trunks, table legs, doorways, lamp stands, sides of houses, fences, windows, picture frames, dressers, chairs, computers, boxes, and coffee cups.

Look up from this book for a moment and see the different vertical directions in your world right now. In your journal, make a list of all the vertical directions that you see. Contemplate the attributes of the vertical directions and edges of things in your world. For example, the attributes of straight and up come to mind right away. How about reaching for the sky, lift, support, alignment, strength? Think about how you feel when you stand up — in good health, independent, confident, positive, capable, secure in your individuality.

What attributes of vertical come to mind for you? List these attributes in your journal. What vertical attributes are evident in your life at this time?

What vertical attributes are not evident in your life at this time?

In the following exercises, you can use 2B or 4B pencils, pens, or even crayons. Whatever you have is fine. I ask my students to use

The artist must train not only his eye, but also his soul.

• • • Wassily Kandinsky

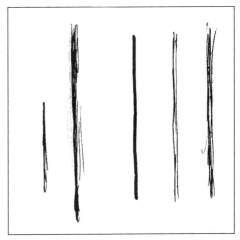

Examples of vertical directions

You can never do too much drawing.

• • • Tintoretto

easy-to-find drawing implements, since everyone carries either a pen or pencil in their purse or pocket. Also a pen or pencil is familiar, thus comfortable, which is important when drawing. I do not want you to feel as if you are doing something strange and exotic when you draw, but rather that you are doing the most natural thing in the world — exploring your world and expressing your heart. I also ask my students to be open to using either hand when drawing. When one hand becomes too tight, too nervous, too tired, use the other.

These very simple warm-up exercises are indispensable to helping you access visual information in the world around you. The drawing exercises that come later ask you to look for things that you have learned about in these warm-ups. Take your time. Read a bit, then put the book down and look for the cues elaborated here. Elevate your drawings from mere exercises to visual experiences.

Objective feeling, view from church patio, ink, 2001

EXERCISE: Vertical Directions

1. Sit. Breathe.
2. Gaze softly at the world before you now.
3. Notice vertical directions: doors, windows, lamps, table legs, fences, walls. What vertical attribute do you need in your life at this time? Confidence? Strength? Good health? Alignment? Independence? A positive attitude?
4. Select something to draw that expresses this attribute.
5. Gently place your pencil on paper. Relax your

wrist, arm, elbow, shoulder. Move your pencil in the same general direction as the vertical edge that you are looking at. As you draw this line, imagine and feel that you are drawing this attribute into yourself.

6. Wherever you go today look at vertical directions and feel this attribute growing in you.

horizontal directions and attributes

No matter where you choose to look you will find horizontal directions: in table tops, the bottoms or tops of picture frames, windows, fences, boxes, skirt hems, some eyebrows, the siding on a house.

Look up from this book for a moment and see the different horizontal directions in your world right now. In your journal, make a list of the horizontal directions that you see. Contemplate the attributes of these horizontal directions. For example, for me, the attributes of lying down, sleeping, and being at peace come to mind right away. A horizontal line often connects two vertical lines, so consider the attributes of communication, connection, sharing, reaching across, integrating, and dialogue. Since vertical is positive, then horizontal is negative. We need both. What attributes of horizontal come to mind for you?

What horizontal attributes are evident in your life at this time?

What horizontal attributes are not evident in your life at this time?

The over-academic education might be leaving out the understanding that:

1. *Book learning is cut off from ordinary living.*
2. *There is too little essential recognition of the essential role of the bridge between lived experience and logical thought: that is, the role of the intuitive image.*
3. *There is not enough recognition of the danger of that too early or too docile acceptance of the public reality that an intellectual statement is.*

• • • Joanna Field,
On Not Being Able to Paint

Examples of horizontal directions

Objective feeling, Vista High School,
ink, 2001

*Living is a form of not being sure, not
knowing what next or how. The moment
you know how, you begin to die a little.
We guess. We may be wrong, but we
take leap after leap in the dark.*

• • • Agnes de Mille

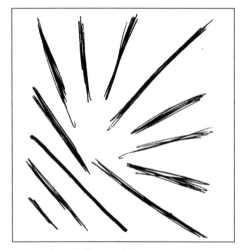

Examples of diagonal directions

EXERCISE:
Horizontal Directions

1. Sit. Breathe.
2. Gaze softly at the world before you now.
3. Notice horizontal directions: table tops, picture frames, boxes, windows, eyebrows. What horizontal attribute do you need in your life at this time? Sleep? Communication? Dialogue? Sharing? Connection?
4. Select something to draw that expresses this attribute.
5. Gently place your pencil on paper. Relax your wrist, arm, elbow, shoulder. Imagine your pen or pencil moving in the same general direction as the horizontal edge you are looking at. As you draw this line, feel that you are drawing this attribute into yourself.
6. Wherever you go today look at the horizontal directions and feel this attribute growing in you.

diagonal directions and attributes

No matter where you choose to look, you will find diagonal directions, in tree trunks leaning to one side, tops and bottoms of open doors, fences and windows seen from an angle, roofs, noses, shoulders, jaws, eyebrows, and, of course, telephone wires stretching far into the distance.

Look up from this book for a moment and see the different diagonal directions in your world right now. In your journal, make a list of the diagonal directions that you see. Contemplate the attributes of the diagonal directions of things in your world. For example, the attribute of being different comes to mind right away. Vertical and horizontal are the norm in 2-D space. Diagonal brings in depth (3-D space) and divergence from the norm. Diagonal is about going and coming, being drawn into, compelled forward, attraction, depth. What attracts you? If nothing attracts you, life feels flat and dull. What attributes of diagonal come to mind for you?

What diagonal attributes are evident in your life at this time?

What diagonal attributes are not evident in your life at this time?

When the world becomes repressive and ugly and mean, we need form and beauty and balance. That's when artists feel most pressed into service.

• • • Dorianne Laux, poet

EXERCISE: Diagonal Directions

1. Sit. Breathe.
2. Gaze softly at the world before you now.
3. Notice diagonal directions: telephone lines, sides of tables, shelves, fences, shoulders, eyebrows. What diagonal attribute do you need in your life at this time? An acceptance of your uniqueness? A willingness to be drawn toward love? Intimacy? Creativity? Depth of feeling? A mission?
4. Select something to draw that expresses this attribute.
5. Gently place your pen or pencil on paper. Relax. Move in the same general direction as what you are looking at. Feel that you are drawing this attribute into yourself as you draw.
6. Wherever you go today look at the diagonal directions and feel this attribute growing in you.

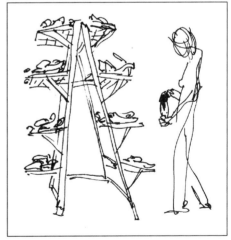

Objective feeling, shoe store at the mall, ink, 2000

Example of familiar form with extended directions

Extended Directions allow you to abstract from physical objects essential information which brings a sense of wholeness to your drawing.

• • • Jan Valentin Saether, from my class notes

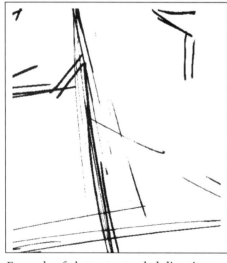

Example of abstract extended directions

extended directions: being willing

Extending the directions helps you to make a structurally sound and proportionately beautiful drawing.

How do you do this? It is easier said than done, of course, yet just being willing to do it works. Begin by drawing the directions that feel accessible to you. Hold your pencil lightly. Loosen your wrists, elbows, and shoulders. Author and art teacher Robert Henri says, "There is a line that runs right through the pointing arm and off from the finger tip into space. This is a principal line — which the artist draws and makes you follow." Does the drawing above express this?

Feel the direction. Is it vertical, horizontal, or diagonal? Feel the weight of it. Do not be concerned with where it begins or ends. Extending the directions allows the form to develop on your paper without you having to exert lots of energy trying to make it happen. Instead, your effort goes into relaxing, opening your heart, and simply being willing to follow the directions that you see.

If you are like most people, a part of you feels that when you draw you must get the form down on the paper exactly the way you see it. You feel you must control the pencil, the process, the outcome. I know, because I struggle with this too. The urge to control and to get the drawing right as quickly as possible — whatever right means — is your left brain trying to draw. Remember: It can't draw. This linear, judgmental, and conceptual part of you has no time or interest in *feeling* the directions; instead, it wants to name, control, organize, and direct them. You have to shift mentally out of your left brain and into your right in order to draw. Extending the directions you see helps you make this shift.

The forms that exist in 3-D space, especially the human body, contain stories. The form of a chair expresses the story of a particular style and era, a particular furniture designer and manufacturer. A memory that goes back to your childhood may be triggered as you draw the chair. When you pay attention to the directions that you see, and when you really *feel* these directions and follow them on paper, the inherent story and Spirit of the form comes alive. You feel this aliveness. Everyone feels it.

You are evoking form, not trapping, capturing, killing, and mounting a form on your paper. You are cocreating a new story — birthing a new form through you and through your unique point of view.

All the drawing exercises in part 1 provide an opportunity for you to honor the veracity and intelligence of both you and the forms before you.

Example of abstract extended directions

EXERCISE: Extended Directions

1. Sit. Breathe.
2. Gaze softly into the world before you.
3. Select a direction to draw, one that feels accessible to you.
4. Hold your pencil loosely. Relax your fingers, wrist, elbow, and shoulder. Loosely draw the direction (vertical, horizontal, or

Example of familiar form and extended directions

Art tends toward balance, order, judgment of relative values, the laws of growth, the economy of living — very good things for anyone to be interested in.

••• Robert Henri, *The Art Spirit*

Objective feeling, Malibu life-drawing class, graphite, 1983

diagonal) just like you did in the previous exercises, only this time extend the line far past where it actually begins and ends. Draw the line again and again until you really feel it.

5. If you feel yourself tightening up, tell yourself it's okay. And relax once again.

6. Now look at the actual line in space — extended through your imagination. What else connects with this line beyond its tangible edges? For now just notice.

intersections: focusing on essentials

An intersection is the place where two directions come together. Focus on this spot and notice its nature.

A story (or Spirit) lives within every form. And every story conveys a feeling. A feeling comes forward and expresses itself on your paper when you focus on intersections. This happens as naturally as butter melts in the sun.

Look at the drawing opposite and see the intersections. Notice the obvious pen lines drawn next to several of the actual but subtle intersections. Do you see what I mean by intersection now? Each intersection tells you which form comes forward, which goes behind; this expresses depth.

Drawing is a way to sensually connect with the world. Conceptually speaking, we feel separate from the world. We need to find ways to connect without judging, analyzing, dominating. Through your willingness to pay attention to the intersecting areas, the Spirit, story, and feeling of the form flows through your hand. It is a natural union. Think of it as a kind of birth.

Another term for intersection is *anchor point.* Visual information about the form is anchored in the intersection. Feel the nature of the intersection. Notice if a direction is vertical, horizontal, or diagonal, if it is thick or thin, if one side of the line is dark or light. Don't try to be perfect, and don't worry about the exact mathematical degree of the intersection. Engineers are concerned with exact numerical values — artists are concerned with visceral feelings. Numbers won't help you draw — your own visceral feelings will.

Trees may offer the simplest opportunity to work with intersections. When you are just beginning to practice, it is good to select simple subjects. Every branch intersects either the tree trunk or another branch. Little branches intersect bigger branches. If there are leaves on the tree, they hang down or stick out or rise up, and they intersect either the trunk, a branch, other leaves, the fence, the car, the house, or the windowsill.

No matter where you look, you will find intersections. Even shadows can cast strong directions across windows and walls.

Chiaroscuro, an Italian word meaning clear (*chiaro*) and dark (*scuro*), is a technique of using light and shade, without regard to color, that Renaissance artists employed to convey perspective. Forms near you have clear, sharp directions. Forms far away from you have obscure, hazy, indistinct directions.

You have to look, really look, at people and things.

••• Jan Phillips, *Marry Your Muse*

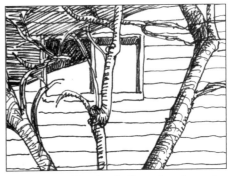

Objective feeling, view from the office window, ink, 2000

Art does not reproduce what we see. It makes us see.

••• Paul Klee

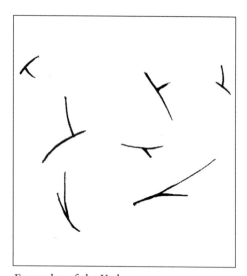

Examples of the Y-shape

EXERCISE: Intersections

1. Sit. Breathe.
2. Gaze softly into the world before you.
3. Find a window. Trees, branches, the neighbor's fence or house, cars, and so on often intersect with the inside edges of windows.
4. Notice the edges of your window and anything that intersects with those edges.
5. Go around the window and make little tic marks to indicate the intersection places.
6. Notice the angles of intersection. Feel these angles and draw the directions out from them. Carefully connect the tic marks around the window.
7. Stand back and appreciate your drawing when you finish.

the visual key to drawing what you see

The visual key to drawing what you see cannot be found in any art book. I got it from Jan Valentin Saether, with whom I apprenticed and with whom I lived, along with his family. One morning before work, I was having breakfast when Jan came to the table mumbling something about a dream he just had. It was a most unusual and compelling dream. His mind's eye was filled with several abstract directions. The intersections were especially pronounced. He couldn't get the dream out of his mind. He didn't know what it meant, though he knew it meant something. But what? One glyph (much like the ABCs of verbal language) was making a large impression on him.

As he painted that day, it became clear to him. This dream was expressing a kind of code! Mr. Saether was devoted to seeing in a very specific way, and he saw something important in this dream that would help him create better paintings. Someone else might have tossed off this dream symbology as meaningless.

In the dream he saw little glyphs made up of two directions that intersected. One direction overlapped the other. The glyph was a Y-shape. The dream displayed hundreds of varieties of this Y-shape, all of which were glowing. What was the significance of this Y-shape?

Look up from this book for a minute. Gaze at the room around you. No matter where you are (a palace or a prison) you will see this shape. Follow one direction up, down, or sideways until you get to another direction that intersects it. Directions form the edges of doors, desks, buildings, lamps. Notice which direction overlaps the other. Draw the two directions, and also draw the intersection. You can! It is very simple. You have just translated a 3-D phenomenon into a 2-D phenomenon. The overlapping direction on the paper corresponds precisely with the object standing in front of the other thing, whatever it is. Conversely, the direction on your paper that ends when it intersects the other direction corresponds precisely with the object that visually goes behind the other one. So here you have the code for accessing visual information in the world before you. Look for the Y-shapes. You'll see that they are everywhere you look. You can draw anything using this

Teachers open the door, but you must enter by yourself.

• • • Chinese proverb

Examples if the Y-shape with shading

Objective feeling, Milwaukee life-drawing workshop, Prismacolor pencil, 1995

code! You do not need special techniques for drawing hair, hands, feet, faces, or tigers' paws. The Y-shape is a code for breaking through conditioned seeing that only lets us see objects that can be named. Even Leonardo could not draw a name; he looked for Y-shapes.

In the English language there are twenty-six letters. First, you learn the ABCs. Next, you form simple words, like *cat* and *dog*. After that, you put words together to form simple sentences and paragraphs. Finally, you are off and running, writing letters and proposals, filling out forms, reading books and newspapers, and expressing your thoughts and feelings. The world opens up.

What about the visual language? You see things but cannot draw them. Why is this? Because you immediately name and label the things you see. You can't draw a name. You can only draw directions and intersections. Look for the Y-shape.

Too often art teachers set up still life arrangements or bring in live models and tell beginners, "Draw!" Those who sit there in wide-eyed terror are told they just don't have talent. If someone put a Chinese book in front of you and told you, "Read!" would you know how to interpret the characters? Would you believe them if they told you that you just don't have talent for reading? Of course not!

constellations: seeing the pattern

Now we are going to stretch a little. Instead of looking for one Y-shape, you will look for two or three at the same time. We'll call this a constellation. A constellation is a group of three or more stars, or this case, intersections. It takes at least three intersections to set up a visual pattern. You will actually feel your brain cells working when you begin to look for three or four intersections at once. Relax occasionally, and instead of zeroing in on just one intersection, back up a bit and focus on three or four at one time. The pattern or constellation is there; you are just not used to seeing it consciously. You will feel different when you look in this way.

Constellations are patterns. A pattern is a consistent, characteristic form, style, or method. Every leaf of every tree grows according to a pattern coded in its cells. The skin cells of your body die every day and new skin cells are born according to a pattern in your DNA.

In astronomy, a constellation is a formation of stars perceived as a figure or design. In fact, the word *stellar* means related to the stars. Con-stella-tion: a pattern of the stars that enables you to make sense out of the night sky. Ships have been navigating by the stars for thousands of years. Artists have navigated their pencils by looking for patterns, or constellations, in the visible world before them.

When you look at the 3-D world with ordinary eyes, you see a variety of objects you can name. When you look with your artist's eye, you see directions, intersections, and constellations that form relationships. You cannot name these relationships, yet you can see, feel, and draw them.

We all reach a point where our drawing is not working because it is too rigid, out of proportion,

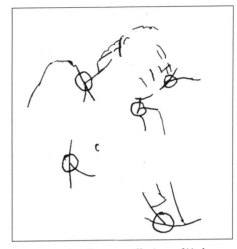

Example of a constellation of Y-shapes

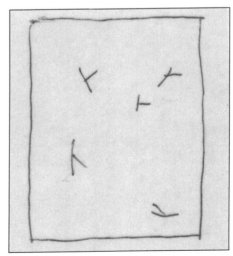

Example of just the Y-shapes

too vague, and so on. Instead of screaming, ripping up your paper, running out of the room, or giving up (all the wonderful tactics we use to avoid and resist our creative expression), there is one very simple thing to do: Go back and look for pattern. Look for directions, intersections, and the Y-shape. Compare the patterns of constellations on your paper with the pattern of constellations on the object, figure, or landscape. Y-shapes are like the information booth at a mall: You go there when you are lost or looking for a particular store. If you feel lost while drawing, and goodness knows it happens a lot for me, head straight for the Y-shapes and compare yours with what is in front of you. It is easy to correct a drawing by adjusting the Y-shapes and redrawing the directions. Extra lines often add a very nice flavor to a drawing.

Think about your energy. It takes an enormous amount of energy to conquer something. It takes a different kind of energy to look for the pattern, make connections, see relationships. It feels good to accept your point of view exactly as it is.

Relax and allow your hand and pencil to follow what your eye sees. You will be rewarded with a drawing that looks and feels as if it is breathing with a life of its own. What was once just marks on paper suddenly becomes alive with depth, meaning, feeling, and a unique story.

Objective feeling, Eduardo, graphite, 1984

EXERCISE: Constellations

1. Sit. Breathe.
2. Gaze softly into the world before you.

3. Sit before a window with a variety of directions intersecting the top, bottom, and both sides.

4. Place your first intersection tic mark on the top of the window where a direction intersects it. Look at the bottom of the window and locate a second intersection. Place the second tic mark. Look at the left and right sides of the window and locate a third and fourth intersection, then place the tic marks.

5. Compare the constellation of tic marks on your paper with those on the window. Make adjustments if necessary.

6. Notice the shape of the constellation. Remember, it is always easier to draw when you see the pattern.

Warm-up example

collisions and transitions: flowing with light and dark

So far you have been learning about lines, directions, intersections, and constellations. It is time to learn about light and dark. Specifically, you are going to explore what is called the scale of light. The scale of light is a range of value that runs from blackest black to lightest light. Dark is included as part of the expression of light. Artists use the full scale to express depth, movement, variety, drama, and balance.

In the following exercise you will learn how to make smooth transitions from dark to light. You will also learn to have the light and dark collide. When light and dark collide you have high contrast. It can be almost jolting when the

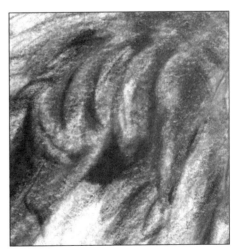

Detail

dark confronts the light. A light may shine down on a tabletop. The tabletop is bright, whereas the side of the table is much darker. The edge between the top and the side marks the collision where light and dark come aggressively against each other.

When light and dark gradually change into one another or blend, you have low contrast, or transitions. Round surfaces, like the trunk and branches of a tree, exhibit transitions. Notice how one side is dark and how gradually the dark transitions into light on the other side. Transitional areas are gentle, peaceful areas.

The scale of light moves smoothly from the darkest dark that your pencil can make to the lightest light of the paper. Your brain interprets the scale of light in very specific ways. Light appears to come toward you, while dark appears to move back and away from you. Forward and backward, toward and away: This duality creates a sense of space, distance, and depth.

Creating contrasts helps you to fabricate distinctions between different forms and to create illusions of depth, dimension, and light.

• • • Judith Cornell,
Drawing the Light from Within

EXERCISE:
Twenty-Minute Warm-Up

1. Breathe. Relax your wrist, arm, elbow, shoulder.
2. Press a soft pencil (4B or ebony) firmly, making heavy, smooth black strokes. Lighten the pressure of the pencil as you proceed to the lightest end of the scale, fading into the white of your paper.
3. Don't be afraid to press hard to make your black really black. Go over it several times. Learn to manipulate your pencil to get the darkest dark possible. Many people do not

go black enough. Don't be timid! Push yourself. See how dark and black you can make the dark end of the scale.

4. Learn to manipulate the muscles of your hand and arm to gradually lighten the pressure of the pencil on the paper. You are creating a smooth transition and a complete scale of light.

Look at a lit lightbulb. Notice how you suddenly squint. The light almost assaults you when you look straight at it. It comes toward you, even into you. In contrast, the dark retreats from you. Look at the shadow beneath the refrigerator or cabinet or look out your window at a dark patch beneath some bushes. Notice how your attention is pulled to this area. The intense dark can be experienced as deep, hidden, mysterious, intriguing, distant, unknown, and sometimes scary and dangerous.

Another expression of the dark-light polarity is reflection and absorption. The white of your paper reflects light. The dark mark of your pencil absorbs light. Judith Cornell uses a wonderful exercise to open the imagination and practice the scale of light. It can be found in her excellent book *Drawing the Light from Within*. With her permission I offer a shorter version of this exercise to you.

Shading establishes mood, tone, and makes things look real, as if they existed in space as 3-dimensional objects. The skill of seeing and drawing lights and shadows is truly joyful.

• • • Betty Edwards,
Drawing on the Right Side of the Brain

Intuitive feeling, trying to free ourselves, ink, 1999

EXERCISE:
Collisions and Transitions

For this exercise use a 4B or ebony pencil, which makes dark, smooth

Collisions and transitions exercise,
graphite, 1999

marks. After you've done the warm-up exercise above, take a sheet of white 12 x 18-inch drawing paper. Draw a 1-inch-wide frame around the edge of the paper. Have on hand a clean sheet of paper to cover areas on which you are working. Rest your hand on this paper to prevent smudging and smearing your drawing.

1. Sit. Breathe.
2. Begin anywhere inside the 1-inch border and use your pencil to make a light scale. Then make another one. And another. Remember to move smoothly from dark to light. Decide where to place the scales by reminding yourself to relax, breathe, open your heart, let go of worrying about doing it perfectly. Work like this for about twenty minutes.
3. At the end of twenty minutes, stand back and look at your drawing. Ask three questions. Did you use a full spectrum of black to white in each scale? Are your scales smoothly blended? Is your black really black? If not, go back and spend some time overlapping and blending so that your eye sees a smooth transition and a rich black.
4. Now slightly change your focus. Look at the scale of light and see if you can make some of the scales thick and some thin, some wide and narrow, some long and short, some curved and square, and some triangular, circular, or random. Avoid copying symbols or objects from the outer world. While drawing, imagine that you are

standing at the very center of your heart, and just feel the energy of this space in you.

5. After twenty minutes of varying the sizes and shapes of the scales of light, stand back and look at your work. Do you still feel that more variety is needed? If so, continue drawing until you feel satisfied.

6. Now slightly change your focus again. This time focus on the empty white areas left on the paper. Look for areas that are beginning to take on the appearance of shapes. You may consider these areas to be just the background; however, now you are going to consider them as foreground or positive shapes. These areas are usually called negative spaces. Now it's time to make some of the negatives into positives. You integrate the negative spaces into the composition by using the scale of light to tone around and away from one or two sides of the white areas. Press firmly at the edge of a white space, gradually lifting as you move away from it. In this way the white areas take on a more definite form. After about twenty minutes stand back and see if both light and dark shapes come forward and also if they retreat into the background.

7. Now see the drawing as a harmonious whole. Is it pleasing to you? Does it feel finished, or have you really just begun? Some people finish quickly. Some are absorbed for hours and hours. You can repeat steps three through six again and again. Smooth out the transitions and intensify the collisions. Think about applying more black over some of the areas on which you have

Work with your pencil or pen putting light and dark together on the same paper. Make mistakes. Be gentle. Be courageous. Explore the possibilities of putting light and dark together and taking them apart. Think of all the positives in your life — all the negative, the good/bad, up/down, difficult/easy, known/unknown. They exist quite beautifully together. And you are more than any one of them for you are the full scale of light.

• • • Helen Wilson

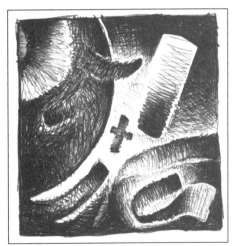

Collision and transitions exercise, ink, 1999

already drawn. Consider ways to overlap and combine smaller, less interesting areas into several larger areas. Make sure you have at least several intense collisions — the white of the paper colliding against the blackest black your pencil can make.

8. At the very end, ask the drawing: What do you need to feel complete? Just listen. Be gentle and kind to yourself. You have just completed your first abstract pencil drawing!

When my students finish a drawing, I always have them put it up on the wall with tape, or I hold it for them. I ask him or her to stand back about 8 to 10 feet and just look at it calmly, to look for a sense of harmony. I say, "Treat the drawing like it is a part of you, for indeed it is, and ask it what it needs to feel complete." There is always a little chuckle, then a shrug, and shortly thereafter, the answer comes. "It could use more dark in that corner." In the figure on page 53, I asked that question several times. For a long time the upper right corner was light. When I finally darkened that corner, the drawing really came to life.

DRAWING EXERCISES

doors: passages in consciousness

Every door leads somewhere. In the drawing on the right, the lobby doors of the hotel lead to an interior courtyard, swimming pool, and guest rooms, while the door in the drawing below clearly leads to a small bathroom.

Doors are easy to understand when drawing. They provide easy-to-see vertical and horizontal directions. Of course, when a door opens toward or away from you, the tops and bottoms form diagonal directions. You do not have to be an engineer to draw these directions. Artists visually feel the angle where one direction intersects another.

Reflect on your life for a moment. Imagine walking down a hallway that has many doors. What door in your life would you like to close? Is it perhaps a door to a limiting belief or an unhealthy relationship? Picture yourself standing before this door. What does it look like? Is it a large heavy iron door, an old wooden door, an ordinary door? Imagine closing this door.

Now walk down the hallway and choose a new door in consciousness — a new belief, a new loving relationship, a good job. Picture yourself standing before the door that leads to this room. What does this door look like? Is it a golden door, a beautifully carved wooden door, or a white picket fence gate? Imagine entering the new room and standing in this new space. What does this space feel like?

Now come back to the present moment.

Objective feeling, Humphrey's lobby, ink, 1999

Objective feeling, guest bathroom, ink, 1999

Looking and seeing both start with sense perception, but there the similarity ends. The purpose of looking is to survive, to cope, to manipulate, to discern what is useful, agreeable, or threatening to the Me, what enhances or what diminishes the Me. When, on the other hand, I SEE, suddenly I am all eyes, I forget this Me, am liberated from it and dive into the reality of what confronts Me, become part of it, participate in it.

• • • Frederick Franck,
The Zen of Seeing

Objective feeling, the counseling center, ink, 1999

Look at the doors around you. Notice directions, intersections, constellations, collisions, and transitions. When drawing something as mundane as the doorway between a counseling room and an office, you will probably see many ordinary things for the first time. For example, in the drawing below I noticed two framed pictures on the wall, vertical blinds, and the surge protector on the floor beneath the desk. Until I sat down to draw, I never saw them. Or perhaps I saw them, but they never registered as important. Though I had picked them up unconsciously, now I am conscious of them. Drawing is one way to make the unconscious more conscious.

It is time for you to go out into the world and look for a door that corresponds with your imagined new room. What kind of door reflects your new chosen belief? Look at the ornate doors of your library, the magnificent doors at a museum, the old, rusty doors on a tool shed. Go to Home Depot and examine French doors, screen doors, front doors. Use doors as a metaphor for a new way of looking at things.

EXERCISE: Drawing a Door

1. Find a door that corresponds with your imagined new room. Sit some distance from it and gaze at it with your artist's eye, looking for directions, extended directions, intersections. What kind of door is it?
2. Relax your tummy, wrist, arm. Breathe.
3. Loosely draw the frame of the door — vertical, diagonal, horizontal. Extend the directions with light lines.

4. Notice intersections. If the door is open, follow the intersections into the new room. Feel that you are actually crossing the threshold and entering this new room.

5. When you finish drawing, give this door a title or name; it can be one word or a phrase.

windows: your outlook on life

The fig tree outside our front window is beginning to produce the second round of fruit. Big black ravens have eaten many figs already.

Windows provide easy access to drawing complex scenes. For example, in the drawing of the fig leaves above right, I first drew the frame. Horizontal and vertical lines are easy. The diagonal telephone line intersects the right edge and extends through both windows.

Beneath the telephone line, a little more than halfway down the right edge of the window is the first leaf. I drew the angle at the top of the leaf where it intersects the window and followed it around to where it joins another leaf beneath it, and so on. A drawing is a process. Seeing drawing this way is a form of prayer. It is a dynamic acceptance of the present moment, a willingness to see everything as it is, complete and perfect. It is a wonderful way to acknowledge the presence of God.

Sit quietly in your chair for a few minutes before leaving the house. Or sit in your car waiting for your child at school. Just sit and look for directions, intersections, collisions, and transitions. While focusing your attention in this way, notice that the chattering mind

Objective feeling, fig tree in late summer, ink, 2000

Objective feeling, palm trees outside my hotel window, ink, 2000

with its many concerns fades into the background. It seems to run on another track; it's not totally gone, it's just not so dominant and demanding. You are freeing yourself to see more of the world around you, which can be a relaxing, expansive, and uplifting experience.

I recommend that you try this the next time you find yourself having anxious thoughts while waiting for your flight at an airport, for example. Sit still, gaze, and look for directions. Marvel at all the intersections. Then take out your paper and pen and draw what you see.

I drew the above left drawing on a long plane ride to Australia. The old man next to me never once looked up from his magazine. It was kind of him to give me the freedom to look at him without his being suspicious, nervous, or self-conscious. Perhaps his eyesight was not good and he didn't even know I was drawing him.

The drawing below left is of what I saw one day through a window overlooking a parking lot at an office where I worked. Drawing helps me feel connected to my world in a deep, gentle, and real way. I do not impose my will on it. I do not feel the urge to make something out of it. I enjoy simply being in this world.

As you know, windows are everywhere: in schools, shops, buses, airplanes, offices, hospitals, and restaurants. Every home has at least one. Windows provide a natural frame that makes it easier to see patterns of directions.

Objective feeling, flight to Australia, ink, 2000

*I question not my physical eye
any more than I would question a
window concerning light.
I look through it and not with it.*

• • • William Blake

Objective feeling, office window overlooking a parking lot, ink, 2000

EXERCISE: Drawing a Window

1. Look up from this book for a moment. Is there a window in the room where you sit

reading? If not, go to another room to do this exercise. Looking at the window, notice what you see through the glass: a tree, another building, people, a bird, a cloud? Is there a telephone wire stretching across the view?

2. Notice what intersects the inner edges of the window (at the right, left, top, and bottom).

3. Relax your tummy, wrist, and arm as you bring your pen or pencil to the paper.

4. Follow the directions with your eye and hand, like a disciple follows a master, like night follows day.

5. When you finish drawing, give your window a title or name.

Objective feeling, items on an office desk, ink, 2000

tables: supporting your interests

You can also find tables everywhere. There are all kinds of them: big, heavy, delicate, graceful, pert, practical, and funky. Have fun looking for them in your surroundings.

The word *table* comes from the Latin *tabula,* or board. A board is just a flat piece of wood on which something happens. Official meetings are often held around the board. A table is essentially a horizontal surface with legs. All kinds of things can be set, served, and displayed on the top of a table. Food, drinks, reading material, fountains, houseplants, knickknacks, lamps, computers, pencil holders, favorite photos — the list is truly endless. We'd be lost without our tables — everything

Objective feeling, Kay Andrews, proofreading, ink, 2000

Objective feeling, office patio tables, ink, 2000

Objective feeling, view in our living room, ink, 2000

would be on the floor! Tables provide support. They lift things off the floor where we can more easily reach them. So the attributes of table are support and lift. What other attributes do tables express?

Look at the horizontal surfaces in your home and office. Look at tables in the park, at a restaurant, at the airport. Notice what kind of things are set on tables, desks, and countertops. Look at tables from above, below, and straight on. The drawing on the left is of a grouping of curved cement patio tables and benches outside an office where I worked for a period of time. Even round tables viewed from above have a horizontal attribute.

Below is a drawing of a round antique ice cream table that sits in our living room. It is covered with a cloth and an aromatherapy candle sits on it. Next to the candle is a thin stone goddess that was given to us as a gift. A large flowerpot with a ficus tree intersects the table, as does the bottom of a standing sculpture and a bit of floor molding.

My energy settles a bit when I draw tables. Vertical lines are grounded with horizontal lines. Objects on a table dutifully and thankfully obey the law of gravity, giving horizontal directions the attributes of peace, groundedness, and stability.

EXERCISE: Drawing a Table

1. Select a table that expresses lift, support, peace, groundedness, or whatever attribute you feel would be helpful to you at this time.

2. Sit down at a little distance from the table and just notice if you are looking down at it, up at it, or whether you are at eye level with it. Check out all three perspectives and choose the one that feels the most comfortable for you to draw.

3. How much of the table can you actually see? If the table is full of books or dishes, some of the table will be visible and some will not. You can only draw what you can see. You are not drawing the table as an isolated object. You are only drawing directions. Each direction expresses an attribute. *Feel* the attribute as you draw the direction.

4. Relax your tummy, wrist, and arm as you bring pen or pencil to the paper.

5. Look for a direction that feels accessible to you. Notice directions that intersect it. Draw what you see. You only have to look for vertical, horizontal, and diagonal directions.

6. Feel the attribute as you draw the direction, for example, support, lift, peace, groundedness.

7. When you finish, give your drawing a name or title. If you feel inspired, write about the attribute or create a story about this table: its creator, owner, history, future, and so on.

chairs: claiming your authority

The chair is an ancient symbol of authority going back to the days when kings and rulers were the only ones who owned chairs. Everyone else stood or squatted. In present times it

Drawing gives one a feeling of power — not power over things or people, but some strange power of understanding or knowing or insight. Or perhaps it is just the power of connection itself. Through drawing, one becomes more connected to things and to people outside oneself, and perhaps it is this strengthened connection which seems to signify personal empowerment.

••• Betty Edwards,
Drawing on the Artist Within

Objective feeling, rattan chair, ink, 2000

is important where you sit. Look what happened when Rosa Parks sat down on the bus in Montgomery, Alabama!

You may want to get out of the house for this drawing exercise, but wherever you decide to go is fine — a sidewalk cafe, an old, stately library, a bench in the park, a furniture store, or even your own bedroom. It may be helpful to choose a place where no one knows you so you can sit alone while you draw with no one approaching you to chat. If someone does talk briefly with you, be courteous and then kindly dismiss them before they settle down next to you. This is your special time for drawing. Smile and return to gazing at a chair that symbolizes authority to you.

The seat of a chair must be somewhat close to horizontal, but the back, legs, and other supportive elements of its design can express vertical as well as a wide assortment of diagonal directions.

Chairs come in an infinite variety of shapes and sizes and styles. Authority also comes in an infinite variety of shapes and sizes and styles. Your own sense of authority and your unique way of expressing it are perfect for you. It might be true to say that just about everyone has problems with authority. Many people do not claim their own authority, and this is mostly because they do not know better. They put authority outside themselves onto others and then spend lots of energy rebelling, resisting, blaming, and complaining. It is a huge step to decide to accept yourself as the authority in your life and to be 100 percent responsible for the quality of your actions, behaviors, and responses to life.

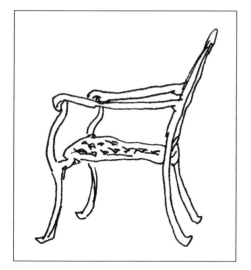

Objective feeling, patio chair, ink, 2000

EXERCISE: Drawing a Chair

1. Select a chair that expresses a sense of authority to you. (It can be new and stylish or old and classic, sporty, comfortable, exotic, or even your favorite, well-worn chair.)

2. Sit a little distance from it and just notice its lines and directions. Select a point of view that feels the most authoritative to you.

3. Relax your tummy, wrist, and arm. Breathe as you bring pen or pencil to the paper.

4. Look for and draw a direction that feels accessible to you. Notice intersections and shapes between the intersections. Draw the constellations you see. Draw negative shapes (empty spaces) between the legs and arms.

5. Feel the attribute of authority as you draw the chair. Imagine yourself settling comfortably into a new and expanded sense of authority that feels appropriate to you. What does this feel like?

6. When you finish, give your drawing a name or title. If you feel inspired, write about the attribute or create a story about this particular chair: Who created it? Who purchased it? Who has sat in it?

Objective feeling, sheet draped behind canvas, graphite, 1983

clothing and drapery: roles to play

Clothing, curtains, drapery, pillows, mattresses, old sheets twisted and turned — these materials lend themselves to the artist's eye.

Objective feeling, copy of Leonardo,
Conte crayon, 1983

When you draw clothing or drapery, you will find that it is quite easy to shift out of conceptual, left-brain thinking. This is because clothing and drapery are rich with clear directions that cannot be named or labeled. You can see directions and follow them with your eye and hand, yet you don't get stuck in defining anything. It is only cloth, after all.

One day I walked through the studio and saw this very ordinary yet beautiful arrangement of lines and directions. It was an old sheet swung around a large canvas, and the arrangement of its lines expressed a tremendous balled-up energy that had poignant meaning for me at that moment. I myself felt a balled-up energy inside me. I had to draw! The act of drawing somehow helped me release this feeling.

I loved the contrast between the organic lines of the sheet and the straight lines of the stretcher bars: folds, wrinkles, flowing lines, sagging lines, crumpled corners, bunched-up knots, twisted balls of fabric swung around several sturdy, rigid, wooden bars. What a rich environment for feelings from the heart to emerge and tell their story.

Luckily, fabric is everywhere. On a busy street in winter people walk quickly, coats blowing in the wind, sweaters and scarves wrapped around arms and necks. In summer, you may see sheets blowing in the wind. Observe the pant legs of teenagers. What kind of wrinkles are formed when pants are tight and when they are loose? Express your feelings about the fabric you see around you in a drawing.

EXERCISE: Drawing Drapery

1. Select a light-colored sheet or blanket with no design or pattern. You want to draw the directions of the cloth, not the pattern printed on it.

2. Place the fabric against a simple dark background. Let it fall, fold, and crumple up in simple ways.

3. Place a light above and slightly to the side shining down on the cloth.

4. Sit a little distance from the cloth and just notice lines and directions. Choose a characteristic of this fabric that resembles how you feel at this moment (balled up, fluid and free-flowing, structured and proper, tormented, casual, and so forth).

5. Look for a direction that feels accessible to you. Notice directions that intersect it. Using a pen or pencil, draw what you see. Extend directions and just be willing to flow with them.

6. When you finish, give this drawing a name or title. If you feel inspired, write in your journal about this fabric. Create a story about it. Who created it? Who purchased it? If it is a sheet, who has slept in it? What were their dreams?

There is no tree whose branches are foolish enough to fight among themselves.

••• Native American proverb

Objective feelings, trees by labyrinth at Virginia Beach, ink, 2000

trees: being rooted and reaching out

How do you feel about trees? I once moved into an apartment only because it was on a street that was filled with beautiful tall trees.

So I was in the park, 6ish in the A.M., trying desperately not to get tangled up in Murphys leash, when I looked up and there, in front of my eyes I saw the most beautiful tree. I found myself looking at the light and dark of it and realized that I was looking through the eyes of an artist. It's all L•I•G•H•T!

• • • Babs Smith

Objective feeling, ficus tree, ink, 2000

Have you ever done something like that? Think about experiences you have had with trees. Trees speak to us all the time, silently yet profoundly. Their branches remind us to reach up to the light; their roots remind us to stay grounded; their flexibility and strength in the face of storms remind us to bend during times of stress and turmoil.

They are good listeners too. One day I was distraught about something and went for a walk in nature. I was alone and at one point cried out, "Does anyone understand me?" Odd as it may sound, although I saw only trees and bushes, I felt heard. How silly we are to believe that only people have consciousness! It is everywhere! The resolution to many of our problems is close at hand, if only we would listen a little more to nature. Trees also make excellent subjects for beginners learning to draw. Their lines and directions are clear and simple to see. It seems to me that trees like to be noticed.

Outside the staff lunchroom is a little ficus tree (see the drawing on the left). It is hardly noticed in the coming and going of so many people. The day I sat and drew this tree was a typical day. Everyone else in the lunchroom was busily chatting, reading, and wolfing down sandwiches. I sit still for about fifteen minutes looking at the tree with my artist's eye. I have to admit that until that moment I did not really see or appreciate its sweet, delicate nature. Appreciation develops naturally in the process of drawing.

I began drawing the ficus tree at the intersection of the branch and the sliding glass door. Vertical lines are the easiest directions to see and understand. Horizontal lines are fairly easy too. Synthetic objects like doors and windows offer an easy place to begin, because their edges are straight.

The drawing on page 63 is of a pair of curved trees at the Association for Research and Enlightenment (A.R.E.) in Virginia Beach. I was with a group of teachers and had a few minutes before we headed back to the classroom. Drawings refresh your memories, sometimes more pleasantly than images made by digital cameras, video recorders, and so on. The drawing at the right is of a tree that was growing in an abandoned area behind several commercial buildings. Employees parked their cars in front of this tree every day for years. I wonder if anyone ever really saw the tree. One day I sat there sketching lines on my paper, and this lovely drawing emerged.

Is there an unloved, neglected area in your neighborhood? Sit down for a few minutes and just follow the directions that you see before you. Draw only the major directions that feel clear and obvious to you. Let the rest fall into place.

Even a scrappy bunch of twigs and bushes can reveal hidden beauty and cause a genuine feeling of empathy to rise up in you. Feeling empathy can renew your heart and soul, and this renewal will carry you through the day. Your artist's eye is an essential part of transforming the consciousness of humanity. Of course, you have to use it to experience its transforming properties.

Come forth into the light of things, let nature be your teacher.

••• William Wordsworth

Objective feeling, trees and bushes behind office, ink, 2000

Remove your sandals, for the place where you are standing is holy ground.

••• Exodus 3:5

Objective feeling, view behind Hay House, ink, 2000

No matter where I live, I always try to make friends with a tree.

• • • Kent Nerburn, *Small Graces*

Objective feeling, eucalyptus tree, ink, 2000

San Diego County has enjoyed imported eucalyptus trees for nearly one hundred years. This year a virus of some kind is covering the leaves with drops of a gluelike substance, preventing the trees from breathing properly. My heart aches for these lovely trees, many of which have already died. Biologists imported an Australian wasp that we hope will eat this glue and save the trees.

The two drawings on this page tell the story of branches that droop and leaves that curl and wilt. The top drawing began as a challenge. I sat on a bench at the edge of a cliff overlooking a valley. I was taking a break during an assignment and had my sketchbook. I thought about drawing but initially was overwhelmed. This was an immense spatial vista with countless tiny bits of distant visual information. Where to begin?

I sat quietly for just a few seconds. Then I noticed the strong diagonal lines of the branches growing very close to me, extending from left to right across my field of vision. I could draw these clear diagonal lines!

It was easy to place the long, slim diagonal lines of the branches on my paper. I indicated the frame or boundary for the drawing, and from there it was easy to place lines that intersected these strong diagonal lines. Within a few minutes I had a satisfactory arrangement of lines on paper that felt close to what I was looking at. I checked the pattern of constellations and finished up with collisions and transitions (darks and lights).

The drawing on the next page is a composite drawing of a real tree and an imaginary shadow of a tree made with squiggly lines in the form of a wide cross. I felt that the little tree was very pale on the paper and needed something strong to contrast with it. The dark shape behind it helps it to stand out and be strong.

EXERCISE: Drawing a Tree

1. Select a tree that expresses qualities that interest you: a sturdy oak tree, a flexible birch, a friendly ficus, a modest maple, a proud peach.

2. Sit a little distance from it and just notice lines and directions. Choose a point of view that exhibits lines and directions that feel accessible to you.

3. Relax your wrist and arm and breathe.

4. Very lightly draw a direction that feels accessible to you. Extend the direction lightly and notice where one or more directions intersect this one line. Trees have an abundance of intersections that are generally very easy to see and draw. Indicate the intersecting places (anchor points or Y-shapes) with a slightly darker mark. See the patterns or constellations.

5. Compare your constellations with those of the tree in front of you. Adjust wherever necessary.

6. Notice dark and light — collisions and transitions. Usually one side of the tree trunk will be darker, the other side lighter. The same is true of branches. Indicate what you see.

7. When you finish, give your drawing a name

As my pen follows the trunk, I feel the sap rise through it from roots to spreading branches. I feel in my toes how roots grip earth. In the muscles of my torso I feel the tree's upward groping, its twisting, struggling, its reaching against all resistances, toward the sun. In my arms I sense how the branches must wrest themselves away from the parental trunk, to find their own way.

• • • Frederick Franck, *The Zen of Seeing*

Objective and intuitive feelings combined, slim tree with wide cross, ink, 1999

Every movement in nature is orderly, one thing the outcome of another, a matter of constructive, growing force. We live our lives in tune with nature when we are happy, and all our misery is the result of our effort to dictate against nature.

• • • Robert Henri, *The Art Spirit*

Vase of flowers in hotel lobby, ink, 2000

or title. If you feel inspired, write in your journal about this tree. Create a story about it. Who planted it? Who climbed it?

plants and flowers: your growth and blossoming

In what area of your life are you growing and blossoming at this time (career, marriage, creative expression, health, relationships, financial security)?
What kind of soil do you grow best in (positive, truthful, inspired, loving thoughts)?
How much sun do you need (unconditional love and warm attention from friends, coworkers, and family — and from yourself!)?
How much water do you need (emotional support, someone, including you, who believes in you and your abilities and your potential)?

Glance around you as you walk to your car or to the train station. Plants and flowers grow just about everywhere: in the park, between cracks in the sidewalk, along the freeway, at the library, behind the gas station, in front of the hotel, right outside your door. When you draw a flower, you see many petals, leaves, branches, stems, and background material hanging down or sticking out. You may wonder where to begin.

First, allow yourself to be drawn to some part of the plant or flower that interests you — the largest bud on a Christmas cactus, a palm tree reaching to the sky, the thorny stem of a rose. You will be able to see a direction of some kind, and this is the first line that you will put

Plant with lots of leaves, ink, 2001

down on paper. When you look again, you will see other directions intersecting the first one. Indicate those intersections and continue until you feel content and satisfied.

Flowers, vegetables, herbs, trees, ground cover, and bushes all offer a beautiful way to contemplate your own growth and blossoming. Houseplants, low bushes outside the office, a rose from the neighbor's garden — everything that grows expresses the complete cycle of life. We are all budding, blossoming, and taking form according to some inner design, then fading and dissolving back into eternal formlessness where everything, including you and me, eventually return.

Each plant has qualities and characteristics that mirror your life. Think of your life when you draw a flower or a plant. Ask yourself the questions again.

A plant needs three simple ingredients to grow and blossom and fulfill its destiny: soil, water, and sunshine. Every human being needs simple ingredients too: an understanding of the truth, unconditional love, and recognition of your worthiness.

EXERCISE:
Drawing Plants and Flowers

1. Select a plant or flower. Sit before it and just notice lines and directions. Choose a point of view.
2. Relax your wrist and arm. Breathe.
3. With pen or pencil, lightly draw a direction. Extend this line very lightly. Notice what intersects this line. Continue

You know, Charlie, if I told the world how I really got my theory of Relativity they would lock me up.... I was sitting in my garden and my flowers told me.

• • • Albert Einstein to his friend Charles Hapgood

Rose and wicker at the edge of the kitchen table, ink, 2000

We don't see things as they are. We see things as we are.

• • • Anaïs Nin

drawing directions. Indicate intersections with a slightly darker mark. Check for constellations.

4. Compare the patterns of your drawing with the patterns of the plant or flower.
5. Notice and indicate the dark and light, or collisions and transitions.
6. When you finish, give your drawing a name or title. If inspired, create a story about your blossoming.

View across Del Mar racetrack, ink, 1998

distant hills: broadening your perspectives

Waiting for the Del Mar horse race to begin, I drew the distant hills, trees, scattered buildings and grasses pictured top left, while my friends ordered food and drinks, read the program, and penciled in their bets.

I enjoy going places with my friends; however, instead of doing exactly what they do all the time, I do my own thing some of the time. It is very tempting to believe that you have to be part of everything. If they eat, you eat. If they play softball, you play softball. If they discuss the horses, you discuss the horses. Your sketchbook makes it easy for you to go along with your friends and do your own thing!

How do you draw things that are very distant from you? The answer is that you look at distant hills in the same way that you look at everything else when you draw — you notice directions, intersections, constellations, collisions, transitions. Objects in the foreground have sharper edges, clearer lines, and greater

Hills from balcony of office, ink, 1998

contrasts of light and dark. Objects in the distance have softer edges, fuzzy lines, and much less contrast between light and dark.

Distance is expressed very well with low contrast or transitions — everything is muted. A pencil can make soft, gray lines. However, sometimes you don't have a pencil, but you do have a pen. What then? First, select the direction with the greatest contrast. Draw it holding the pen loosely. Make gentle rather than heavy marks everywhere you draw. At the end of the drawing look carefully at the scene before you. Indicate one or two high-contrast areas. Squinting is always helpful. When you squint, the darks and lights stand out, isolating them from all the other areas. This makes it much easier to draw.

The top drawing on the previous page began with the center tree. Once I drew that tree, the other directions related to it. The drawing beneath began with the closest tree. I placed the hills and other trees in relationship to it. The drawing on this page began with the diagonal sloping hill. That direction felt the clearest to me when I first began. All the other marks fell in place on the paper in relationship to that one clear diagonal direction.

Remember, when you are drawing distant things you do not want to define anything too sharply. Also, be sparing with your use of darks, because darks define things. In the distance you just can't see clear definitions. Finally, it does not really matter where you begin a drawing or what you choose to draw first. Keep it simple, and begin with the direction that feels clear, safe, and accessible.

Surrender means the decision to stop fighting the world, and to start loving it instead.

• • • Marianne Williamson

Hills behind Hay House, ink, 1998

Rhinoceros at the zoo, ink, 2001

Antelope at the zoo, ink, 2001

EXERCISE:
Drawing Distant Hills

1. Sit before a distant view of hills. Squint. Notice directions that stand out.
2. Relax your wrist and arm. Breathe.
3. Using a pen or a pencil, lightly draw one direction. Extend this line very lightly. Notice what intersects this line. Continue drawing directions. Indicate intersections (anchor points or Y-shapes) with a slightly darker mark.
4. Compare the patterns on your drawing with the patterns before you.
5. Notice and indicate the dark and light, or collisions and transitions.
6. When you finish, give your drawing a name or title. If inspired, create a story about how you are broadening your perspectives or seeing the big picture of your life.

animals: lessons in unconditional love

When you focus on an animal, your heart naturally opens. For this reason, animals make wonderful subjects.

Though many animals move quickly much of the time, every animal sits or stands or lies down quietly at some point. I'm sure you can find such a moment to share with the animal of your choice. You may choose to draw a dog, cat, toad, lizard, bird, fish, rabbit, hamster, turtle, or guinea pig. You may decide to go to the zoo and draw a monkey, tiger, giraffe, kangaroo, ele-phant, cheetah, wild boar, panda, or zebra. Or you may decide to go to the farm and draw a cow, horse, goat, goose, duck, pig, or sheep. Ani-mals are everywhere! This drawing exercise will go with you wherever you want to go. It will help you look at animals in a new way. Many artists use photographs to work with animals, and you can certainly do this too if you wish.

Scribbling is a good way to draw an animal. In art classes this is called gesture drawing, and it is a highly respectable way to express the activity of any moving form — especially an animal. A few lines express the whole thing: the slow turning of the rhinoceros's head, the pres-sure of the cat's light body as it spreads out on the ground, the stretching of the horse's neck as it reaches for grass, the perky bobbing of the birds as they chatter on the ground.

Keep your lines simple. Feel a heart con-nection with the animal as you move your pencil on the paper.

Animals have a high emotional intelligence — possibly higher or more developed than that of many people. Their instincts, which are inborn patterns of behavior in each species that help them respond to their environment, are especially strong.

If you want to learn about unconditional love, I recommend highly that you get a pet. Dogs and cats are especially capable of teach-ing you how to love. They will look into your eyes with pure love when you feel sad. They love you when you have just been laid off, if your lipstick is smudged, if your ice cream dripped on your shirt.

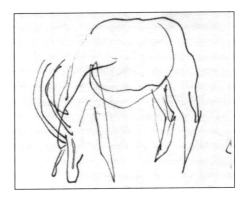

Katie and Kewaska, Humphrey, birds, and a horse, ink, 2000

Find the big shape of the head. All the small bumps are but variations under control of the big shape. This is constructive drawing.

• • • Robert Henri, *The Art Spirit*

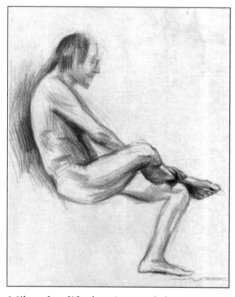

Milwaukee life-drawing workshop, Prismacolor pencil, 1998

As one of my students said, "I don't think I ever actually looked at anyone's face before I started drawing. Now, the oddest thing is that everyone looks beautiful to me."

• • • Betty Edwards, *Drawing on the Artist Within*

EXERCISE : Drawing Animals

1. Choose an animal and sit down with your sketchbook. Squint. Notice directions.
2. Relax your wrist and arm. Breathe. Feel unconditional love between you and the animal.
3. With pen or pencil, scribble a circle to position the head on the paper. Scribble a circle or shape for their body. Scribble legs if you see them. Notice intersections.
4. Compare your pattern of intersections with the pattern on the animal. Adjust your paper if necessary.
5. When you finish, give your drawing a name or title. If inspired, create a story about how you are learning to love yourself unconditionally.

introduction to drawing the human form

The drawings in this book reflect thousands of hours and more than fifty years of drawing. I imagine it is pretty clear that I love drawing the human being more than just about anything else. The essential qualities of a person — feelings, attitudes, character — become visible as you learn what to look for and how to see.

Don't worry about drawing a person. Just draw the directions you see.

I love drawing the directions that express the contour of muscles, bones, and rounded fleshy areas. I love the glistening shapes of highlights. I love constructing and arranging lines and shapes to communicate a human feeling on paper. I love accenting the dark and light areas. I feel as if I am giving birth to something, and perhaps it is for this reason that I feel a little more alive when I draw. I feel responsible (almost like a parent) for loving these drawings into existence and taking care of them, and I am so happy that they are finding their way into the world through this book.

Milwaukee life-drawing workshop, Prismacolor pencil, 1998

I know that not everyone reading this book is as interested in drawing the human form as I am, and that is okay. The human form is a complex arrangement yet it is still just directions and intersections, collisions and transitions. Drawing the human form works best when you feel the directions that you are seeing and drawing.

Your artist's eye knows how to look at the human form with unconditional love. If you are looking with lust or prejudice and bias, it is not the same experience, and your drawing will express these feelings. Unconditional love is a tall order for anyone. It is important for all of us and a necessity for the artist. Looking for directions and intersections is a simple way to see beyond stereotypes, prejudice, judgments, criticism, and old beliefs.

You are not a blank slate when you draw. Much gets stirred up in you when you sit with your drawing board before an unclothed human being. You have to learn how to put your own biases and convictions about people on

Milwaukee life-drawing workshop, Prismacolor pencil, 1998

Milwaukee life-drawing workshop,
Prismacolor pencil, 1995

the back burner. You have to learn to focus on just seeing directions.

Seeing directions and intersections of a particular individual's body is a decidedly delightful way to see the impersonal character of that person. No judgment — just lines. The impersonal aspect of a person is their animating force or Spirit. It comes through in the posture, the slight turn of the head, the puzzled look on the face, the tense arch of the back. The animating force is expressed through the emotions, memory, and convictions of a person. Don't try to fix, heal, alter, or change someone's feelings, even if that person is sad, angry, sick, unhappy, or frustrated. Do not ignore their feelings either. Just draw the directions. Draw the directions and intersections that you see — and lo and behold — the powerful animating force (Spirit or impersonal self) of the person will appear on your paper. A real feeling expressed through drawing is beautiful. You do not have to draw like me or anyone else. The real feeling will be your own!

Fear, hatred, judgment, criticism — these limiting attitudes have no place in an artist's work. Artists work hard to see the Soul of the person they are drawing or painting. Looking at another human being in a new way can be enormously energizing. It can be an effective and powerful way to open your heart to yourself with unconditional love. It can be a safe and enjoyable way to accept yourself at a deeper level than ever before.

hands and feet: standing up and handling life

Hands are miraculous instruments helping you to handle many things. Feet allow you to stand, walk, and run. Seldom do you see a hand or foot isolated from the body, separate, like an apple sitting on a table. Approach drawing hands and feet by seeing them as part of a larger field of intersections.

A profound order exists in the most ordinary places. Every person senses this order. The artist's eye in you can see it and draw it. Be willing to see proportion and order through your own eyes.

No one can draw hands or feet using conceptual thinking! Forget fingers, toes, knuckles, wrists, anklebones, thumbs, and any other part you can name. You absolutely must use perceptual thinking — directions, intersections, constellations, and so on. Extended directions help you place hands and feet in proper relationship with shoulders and head.

Do hands express emotions? You bet they do! For example, the hands of the woman in the drawing to the left (page 76) express hesitation, possibly insecurity, while the hands of the man in the drawing on the next page express that he is withholding his emotions. Hands convey feelings brilliantly. Feet and legs do too. Notice how the woman in the drawing at the right appears ready to get up and go. Her fingers and toes are bent, pressing down on the piano bench and ready to raise the body. Some conviction, belief, or emotion is clearly tensing

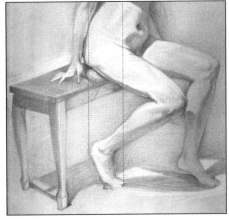

Malibu life-drawing workshop, graphite, 1985

Copy of Velasquez, ink, 1994

the muscles and preparing the body for some kind of movement.

Hold a pencil vertically between your eye and the model. Notice what body parts intersect this line. For example, notice that the heel of the foot and the top hand of the woman in the drawing are on the same vertical line. The toe is on the same vertical line as the intersection of the leg with the piano bench.

Some people draw with ease, while others struggle to see vertical, horizontal, and diagonal. However, everyone benefits by having a genuine and personally meaningful dialogue with the world as he or she sees it. By doing the exercises in this book, you become more conscious of your world, more capable of engaging it and enjoying it — whether or not you consider yourself an artist. You certainly do not have to be an artist to see beauty, to see vertical and horizontal directions, to see how things relate.

No matter what you believe about the world around you, perceptually speaking the world is composed of natural connections and organic relationships. Even when things appear to be unrelated, disorganized, disproportionate, or falling apart, when you draw the mess, you see that all the pieces are proportionately related to other things around them.

EXERCISE:
Drawing Hands and Feet

1. Have a friend agree to sit still while you draw their hands and/or feet.
2. Sit before your model. Squint. Notice directions.
3. Relax your wrist and arm. Breathe.

Randall thinking, Prismacolor pencil, 1984

4. Lightly draw one direction, using pen or pencil. Extend this line. Notice what intersects it. Lightly sketch in those directions and others. Indicate intersections with a slightly darker mark.

5. Compare patterns and constellations.

6. Adjust if necessary.

7. Notice and draw darks and lights.

8. When you finish, give your drawing a name or title. If inspired, create a story about how you are handling life and moving forward.

your own face: mirror work

I'm not good enough, pretty enough, handsome enough. I hate my wrinkles, freckles, lips, eyebrows. My nose is too big and I can't draw! How many of us have had these types of thoughts? Let this exercise help you move beyond your own harsh judgments of yourself.

I once taught a self-portrait drawing class at the University of Wisconsin to people who wanted to learn to draw. We met twice a week for six weeks. Students were amazed at how well they were able to draw using my simple methods of seeing directions and intersections. Of course, we also played gentle music, spoke kindly to ourselves in the mirror, and opened our hearts.

Ah, the mirror. We all encounter the negative messages we send ourselves when we look into the mirror. While drawing your own face, just notice those messages and say, "Thank you for sharing." It is an old tape playing. You are going to make a new mental and emotional tape recording, using a pencil and lots of love.

Self-portrait at age twenty-one, graphite

Self-portrait at age thirty-six,
Prismacolor pencil

The unexplainable thing in nature that makes me feel the world is so big, far beyond my understanding — to understand maybe by trying to put it into form. To find the feeling of infinity on the horizon line or just over the next hill.

• • • Georgia O'Keeffe

Self-portrait at age forty-five, graphite

That your world is in agony is no reason to turn your back on it or to try to escape into private spiritual pursuits. Rilke reminded me that I had the strength and courage to walk out into the world as into my own heart and to love the things as no one has thought to love them.

• • • Joanna Macy, *Rilke's Book of Hours*

Your own face is a wonderful configuration of directions and intersections. Other benefits of drawing a self-portrait are that there is no model fee, no waiting for the model to show up, no need to say, "Please stay in position." It is also a good opportunity to have a little chat with yourself, saying such things as "I love you. I trust you."

At age forty-five, I began criticizing myself for having wrinkles. I decided to do a self-portrait and work with this criticism. My method was to draw, and whenever I became aware of thoughts that were critical, harsh, and judgmental, I stopped drawing, looked with love into my eyes, and said sincerely to myself, "I trust you." I said this until I relaxed and believed it. Then I began drawing once more. This exercise led to a major breakthrough in my life: I met my life partner shortly afterward.

Everyone benefits when you speak kindly, gently, and lovingly to yourself!

EXERCISE:
Drawing a Self-Portrait

1. Sit before a mirror. Gaze and relax. Look into your own eyes and say, "I am willing to learn to love you. I trust you." Or use any positive words you like. Listen with your heart. When you hear your thoughts becoming critical, look into your eyes and repeat those words.

2. Using a 2B pencil, draw a very light, loose circle for your head. Draw one side of your neck with a very light, loose vertical or slightly diagonal line. Extend the vertical

direction in your imagination while looking in the mirror, and see what lines up with it. Indicate with light, loose directions where the eyes, nose, mouth, and hair line up. Remember, you are not drawing eyes, nose, mouth, or hair; you are drawing directions (horizontal, diagonal, or vertical).

3. Notice the constellations on your paper and compare them with what you see in the mirror. Make adjustments when necessary. Praise yourself for showing up and doing this exercise. Remind yourself that perfection is not the goal of life, nor is it the goal of this exercise. The goal is to be yourself, to feel connected with what you are looking at, to practice loving and accepting and trusting yourself, to develop the skill of seeing and drawing.

4. Look for the darkest dark places (nostrils, pupils, the line of the mouth, the hair behind your neck or along the side of your face). Place these darks. Now look for the lightest lights. Squint to see them.

5. Write in your journal how you feel about this experience.

another's face: suspending judgment

When I was a little girl, I remember sitting at my mother's desk, struggling to draw a face of one of my friends from a photograph. In high school my best friend wanted a boyfriend so much it hurt. I could not get her the boy, but I could create a picture of a cute boy standing at

Cindy sleeping on the plane,
Prismacolor pencil, 1995

Suzanne, graphite, 1982

the end of a pier waiting for her. She cried when I presented it to her one day after school.

We look at faces every day. It is time to see a face without fear, agenda, old conditioning, or judgment. It is time to see faces with love.

The dictionary defines the word *face* as 1) value or standing in the eyes of others; prestige. 2) Self-assurance; confidence. A face expresses so much about a person — his or her feelings, sense of confidence, intelligence, motivation, the capacity to learn, openness to listening to what you have to say. People who know how to look can read a person's face (and body language) as if it were an open book.

You study a face for a long time when you draw. The artist's eye does not look at faces like an analyst or doctor looking for signs of illness. Nor does the artist's eye look at faces like an anthropologist looking for ancestral qualities. Fashion designers look for trends. Venture capitalists look for profit. Criminals look for easy targets. Teachers look to see if students are paying attention. Of course, there are many ways to look at faces, and we all employ many methods of seeing in our daily lives.

The artist's eye does not care a whit about fashion, profitability, or racial background. It seeks to see the soul of the person. The artist's eye sees unconditionally. Although everyone has the ability to see without judgment, this ability is seldom, if ever, talked about. "This [artist's] eye is the lens of my heart, open to the world which is fully alive," says Frederick Franck so beautifully.

When you draw a face, you have to learn how to let thoughts, feelings, and judgments

My dad, Prismacolor pencil, 1993

about this person swirl around in the back of your mind like traffic on a busy street. Just because you draw something does not mean your mind stops. Exert just a little bit of control, and you will find it almost easy to focus your attention on directions, extended directions, and intersections.

What is your task when you draw a face? It is to bring forth a feeling of that person's inner being — their essential character. The inner aspects of a person come forward when the artist (you) is motivated by empathy and compassion. Eyes, eyebrows, corners of mouths, a slight turn of the head — all convey the state of the soul. This essential information is there before your eyes. You know what to look for: directions, extended directions, intersections, constellations, collisions, and transitions.

I taught drawing in the Milwaukee County Jail for four years. I like to work with people who live on the fringes (inmates, the homeless, poor people, those in recovery from drugs and alcohol, people dealing with mental or emotional illness, people searching for spiritual truth). All people are interesting to me. Drawing is a safe way for me to interact on many levels with a person.

On page 81 is a profile I drew of my friend Cindy while she was sitting next to me on a plane trip. This drawing, done while she slept, probably took about fifteen to twenty minutes. I have discovered that drawing is a safe way for me to interact on many levels with a person. The front page of the *Los Angeles Times* ran a photo of an Indian boy the day Mother Teresa died (see drawing on page 23). I do not draw

Louise Hay's assistant, Prismacolor pencil, 1995

Often have I heard you say, "He who works in marble, and finds the shape of his own soul in the stone, is nobler than he who plows the soil. And he who seizes the rainbow to lay it on a cloth in the likeness of man, is more than he who makes the sandals for our feet."

But I say that the wind speaks not more sweetly to the giant oaks than to the least of all blades of grass. And he alone is great who turns the voice of the wind into a song made sweeter by his own loving.

• • • Kahlil Gibran, *The Prophet*

Milwaukee life-drawing workshop, Prismacolor pencil, 1994

photographs much, although there was a period when I copied Old Master drawings from photographs in books. It can be easier to draw from a photograph, because the visual information is already translated from 3-D space onto a 2-D piece of paper.

The man depicted on page 82 is my father a few weeks before he died. We had been sitting at my sister's kitchen table for some time after dinner, and luckily I had my sketchbook with me. The woman on page 83 was the assistant to Louise Hay when I worked at Hay House. The young man portrayed on this page was a model in a Milwaukee drawing workshop I attended. Looking at people in an impersonal and unconditional way frees me up inside. It feels very good. And when a drawing feels as if it is breathing with its own life, I feel uplifted.

I tell my students to go to public places and be people watchers. Go to sports events and observe. Look at the people you work with. Look at the faces of your family members. Go to libraries, shopping malls, airports.

One hundred or so years ago, Einstein said we have to change the way we think. His message is still true today. Since drawing uses a different part of the brain than what we usually use, it seems obvious that you can use drawing to change the way you think. Of course, you can change the way you think in many ways. Drawing is one way. It is a playful, safe, relevant, and beautiful way to think differently and to look at life and other people in a new way. It is time to see other people as part of us. Drawing another's face and suspending judgment can be very uplifting.

EXERCISE: Drawing a Portrait

1. Choose either a photograph with clear light and dark shapes and shadows, or find a friend to be a model for you.

2. Sit, gaze, relax, and breathe. Silently say kind, loving words to this person.

3. Using a pen or pencil, lightly draw a very light, loose circle to indicate the head and position the drawing on your paper.

4. Draw a direction that feels accessible and locate another direction that intersects it. I often start with the intersecting directions of the neck and jaw. Very lightly extend an imaginary vertical line through the intersection and notice any other intersections, like eyes, nose, mouth, shoulder, and armpit. Extend an imaginary horizontal line through an intersection and notice other intersections. For example, the top of the ear is on the same horizontal line as the eyes when seen from straight ahead. Work your way around the entire head this way.

5. Compare constellations on your paper with those on the face before you. Adjust your lines accordingly.

6. Look for the darkest places (nostrils, pupils, the line of the mouth, the hair behind the neck or along the side of her or his face). Place these darks. Now look for the lightest places. Squint to see them. When working with a graphite pencil, you can indicate the lightest areas with your eraser, which works like a pencil in reverse.

7. Write in your journal how you feel about this experience.

Malibu life-drawing workshop,
Prismacolor pencil, 1984

the human form: seeing with compassion

Learning to see with compassion is an enormous step for anyone to take. Like everything that is really important, compassion does not happen all at once. It is a deep spiritual feeling that emerges naturally when you let go of some of your old conditioning. It is an unfolding process, and it takes practice. It helps to be really gentle with yourself as you take this step.

Unconditional love is the key to drawing the human form. The artist's eye is capable of seeing unconditionally, which means that it is capable of extracting the abstract qualities of Spirit from the concrete form of the body. Unconditional love is natural; it is inside you right now.

Not everyone who labels him- or herself an artist employs the artist's eye of which I am speaking. It is not an elite eye that exists in only a few chosen people. Rather, it is a powerful potential that exists within the heart and mind of every person. Your artist's eye is activated when you relinquish or give up your need to label and judge things harshly. Soften your eyes. Open your heart. Then you will begin to see things differently.

Every person on the earth sees the world from his or her point of view, and this point of view is completely unique. Like a fingerprint or a DNA map, your perspective is unlike anyone else's. Trust your eyes. Let go of fads, fashions, and the politics of the art market.

Search out masters who appeal to you and copy their lines to learn how they saw and felt.

The artist participates in the production of works which are indications of the work of God.

• • • Paul Klee

Milwaukee life-drawing workshop,
Prismacolor pencil, 1995

You will discover yourself in the process. You, too, can see the Spirit within the form. There are many ways to express your compassion. Search out the ways that appeal to you. You are responsible for drawing out your own way of seeing. No one can do it for you. Your way is good enough.

Generosity and compassion attract the Spirit of a form. Harsh judgments, criticism, labeling, and stereotyping repel the Spirit. Begin every drawing session with a wave of generous compassion first for yourself, feeling it in your body flowing through your blood, stream. Then feel it overflow and extend out to the human forms that share space with you.

When Spirit has been shut out of the process, a drawing is missing something. Even if a drawing is technically perfect, if there is no Spirit, there is no life in the lines or in the drawing. When you look down at your paper and see a lifeless drawing, do not lose hope. Take one minute to put your pencil down, close your eyes, and drop in to your heart. Invite a generous wave of compassion to flow through you once again. When you open your eyes, return your attention to directions and inter-sections. In this way you draw life and Spirit back into the drawing.

Some religions teach their members to see the body as sinful, causing painful misunder-standing. Granted, the natural good and origi-nal blessing with which every baby is born becomes covered over with layers of condition-ing, leading the child to believe that it is not good enough. This core belief opens the door to conflicted emotions and much pain. The

In the oceanic feeling what occurs is a spontaneous expansion of consciousness through which natural phenomena acquire an unaccustomed depth, become charged with meaning, seem to lose their separateness both from each other and their observer, and appear in all their intense relatedness. . . . This is what Coleridge called overcoming "the lethargy of custom."

• • • Andreas Suchantke, *Eco-Geography*

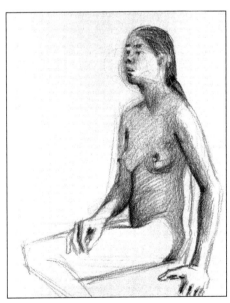

Milwaukee life-drawing workshop,
Prismacolor pencil, 1995

Are you looking for me? I am in the next seat. My shoulder is against yours.

• • • Kabir

West Hollywood life-drawing workshop, graphite, 1998

spiritual journey for everyone is to return in consciousness to the core of original good (Beingness) that exists beneath the conditioning. Is it possible to draw out this goodness and let it be expressed in your life? Yes. You can do this in many ways. Drawing as a sacred activity is one way.

To master something feels wonderful. It probably does not matter what you master; it only matters that it be something close to your heart. Cooking, gardening, carpentry, drawing: What do you love above all else?

I wrote this book to help ordinary people develop the skill of drawing as a way of exploring and getting to know themselves and the world around them. Some readers have a love of drawing and will pursue it till they master it. So let me take a moment here to say a few words about mastery.

When I completed my five-year apprenticeship in 1984, I gave myself a six-week trip to Europe, staying with a friend who had an apartment in Florence, Italy. I ran out every day and got lost deliberately so that I could discover something new in this grand city of art. Out of many experiences, I will share one enormous discovery that helped me to understand something very important.

In a small room of the Uffizi Gallery I stood before five paintings of the annunciation — paintings by Leonardo da Vinci, Sandro Botticelli, Lorenzo di Credi, Luca Signorelli, and Giovanni Bizzelli. Each painting is magnificent. Each is also very different. As I looked at these paintings, an understanding swept through me: Mastery is a willingness to follow your heart, to accept your unique point of view. Mastery is not about being perfect. Though I already knew this, now I *saw* it.

To master the art of drawing, acquaint yourself with the instruments of your craft: pencils, pens, erasers, papers. Know what to look for: directions, intersections, constellations. Do not burden yourself with feelings that you are not good enough, that you are not perfect, or that your work does not compare with so-and-so's.

Search for the simple constructive forces, like the lines of a suspension bridge. Have purpose in the places where lines stop.

• • • Robert Henri, *The Art Spirit*

EXERCISE:
Drawing the Human Form

1. Ask a friend to sit for you or go to a nearby college that has a life-drawing workshop.
2. Sit with your paper and pencil before your model. Relax your wrists and arms. Breathe.
3. Draw a very light circle to position the head and body on the paper.
4. With pen or pencil, draw a direction that feels accessible to you — the edge of an arm, leg, or the head. Locate another direction that intersects it. Very lightly extend a vertical and horizontal line through the intersection and notice other intersections that define the form. Work your way around the figure in this way.
5. Compare constellations on your paper with those on the form before you. Adjust where necessary.
6. Notice and indicate the dark and light areas (collisions and transitions).
7. Human bodies feel pressure after standing

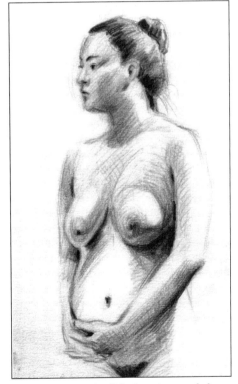

Venice life-drawing workshop,
Prismacolor pencil, 1983

or sitting still for thirty minutes in one position. Where does the model feel this pressure? Mentally feel it in your body. Look at the model; indicate where the pressure is greatest with a line that is a little darker.

NOTE: Whenever you get lost (and you can be assured that you will get lost now and then), just come back to the directions that you see. You can count on them. Check constellations and adjust.

crayons and consciousness

exploring your emotional feelings

Navigating the world exercise (Cindy), ink, 2001

The keystone of emotional intelligence:
Know thyself and be aware of your own feelings as they occur.

• • • Daniel Goleman, author of *Emotional Intelligence*

INTRODUCTION

exploring the interior landscape

The unconscious mind is an undiscovered country, much like America was four hundred years ago. Instead of focusing all your attention on what's happening in the exterior world, once in a while you need to look within.

There are at least three reasons why inner exploration is so valuable. First, it is exciting, because the inner world is a vast and virtually unexplored territory. No one but you can explore your feelings and perceptions. Therapists, ministers, and counselors can be very helpful as you journey inside, but they cannot feel what you feel or see things as you do. You are responsible for your own feelings and perceptions. Even friends who share many of the same feelings and perceptions as you have their own interior landscape to explore. You are an explorer going where no one has gone before.

Second, inner exploration is necessary for problem solving, because the quality of the interior contributes greatly to the quality of the exterior. Every event in the exterior world is held in place by unconscious mental and emotional patterns. Running away from a problem in your marriage, at your job, or with your finances does not work. Living in denial does not work. Beating yourself up for having a problem does not work. Until you go within and change the pattern that creates the outer condition, the same old problem will reappear.

Listening to my beloved inner friend, ink, 2000

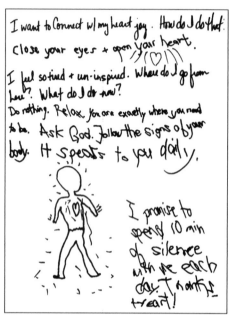

Inner child exercise (Catherine),
crayons, 1995

You can discover more about a person in an hour of play than in a year of conversations.

• • • Plato

Awareness is the first step in freeing yourself from patterns that cause problems in your life. It's enormously helpful to learn that every problem has a solution. Albert Einstein advised us to develop the mind-set that focuses on the solution rather than on the problem. Exploring the interior landscape will help us do just that.

Finally, your health (mental, emotional, and even physical) rests securely on a meaningful dialogue between two aspects of yourself — the interior world of cause and the exterior world of effect. Maintaining good health is vital. Health is balance. If you become off balance (and everyone does now and then), your body and mind naturally try to find their way back to balance. Reestablishing balance is an important skill to develop. I wrote this book to help basically healthy people rebalance themselves emotionally in a playful, imaginative, and visual way: through dialogue and drawing. So let's explore! Sit back, relax, and enjoy the journey.

emotional feelings and the nondominant hand

Just about everyone, including you, has a dominant and a nondominant hand.[*] Are you left-handed or right-handed? If you are left-handed, your left hand is the dominant hand. If you are right-handed, the right hand is the dominant hand. If you are ambidextrous, you are comfortable using both hands; however,

---

[*] I acknowledge the work of Lucia Capacchione for this section of the book. I met Lucia in 1988 in West Hollywood when we both were offering classes free of charge to people with AIDs. Her second book, *The Power of Your Other Hand,* came out that year. Her work with the nondominant hand opened a door in my personal and professional life, for which I am eternally grateful.

you probably favor one hand for writing. What matters here is that you use the hand that is least controlled by your intellect, that you open your heart and feel your feelings.

Which hand feels slow and clumsy when you are writing or drawing? This is your non-dominant hand. You will use this hand to explore your emotional feelings. It is also helpful in exploring your intuitive feelings.

Remember, the nondominant hand did not take penmanship classes and is not skilled in writing or drawing. It cannot write legibly or stay in the lines when you draw. It also cannot instantly do what you tell it to do. It feels weird at first, and it seems to have a mind of its own. Since you do not expect much of it in the way of writing and drawing, it can serve as a kind of open channel for honest feelings straight from your heart.

Drawing with the nondominant hand is a technique that has been used in art classes for many years as a way of loosening up students who tend to get tight and rigid as they try hard to draw what they think they see. The non-dominant hand helps you to relax and draw what you see.

Nondominant hand drawing is childlike. It is a good and safe way to explore the interior world of your emotional feelings, to sort things out, to discover things about yourself, and to access guidance about daily life situations from your inner advisor.

The following example demonstrates how drawing with your nondominant hand can be an effective, quick, and easy form of self-discovery.

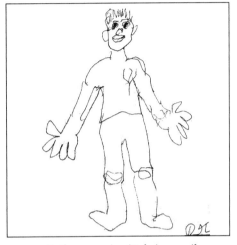

Father exercise (Babs), pencil, 2001

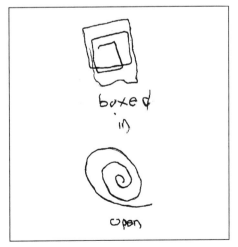

Art is love exercise (Pam), ink, 2000

Pam, a highly intelligent graphic artist, came into my studio one morning looking extremely distressed. She said, "A situation at home is driving me over the edge!"

I did not ask for details. I just asked her to *feel* where this distress was in her body. This took less than five seconds. I asked her if she would be willing to try a little experiment. She shrugged and agreed. I gave her a pencil and paper and asked her to again feel this distress in her body and notice where it was.

I pointed to a piece of blank paper on her desk and asked her to hold the pencil in her nondominant hand. I said, "Imagine the distress flowing from where it is in your body, down your arm, into your hand, into the pencil, and onto the paper. Allow the feeling of distress to make its mark on the paper!" She drew the square spiral (previous page) in about ten seconds.

I said, "Give it a name." With her nondominant hand she wrote, "Boxed in." "Good! Breathe," I said. She looked quizzical, slightly angry, and curious. I continued.

"Now, close your eyes and shift gears. Instead of feeling the distress, I want you to imagine that you are standing at the very center of your heart and feel love. Just *feel love.*"

She did this for about five seconds. "Now, imagine this love flowing into the same part of your body where the distressing situation is." She stood quite still under the skylight for another five seconds.

Finally, I said, "Imagine this love flowing from your heart, down your hand, into the pencil and onto the paper." She drew the bottom spiral in about five seconds. I asked her to

Children paralyzed by fear were quite willing to draw pictures, and thereby communicate what they were feeling and thinking, whereas they steadfastly avoided sustained back and forth talking. Ask your children to draw pictures. That way you' ll really be told about their lives.

• • • Robert Coles,
Drawings and Paintings by Children

name this mark also. With her nondominant hand she wrote "open."

Pam moved from controlled, angular, tight, and very distressed to fluid, open, rhythmical, relaxed, and very surprised — in less than thirty seconds. This change illustrates the ancient truth that the answers to your problems lie within you. Healing is a sacred process of bringing the solution out from deep within.

This analysis is not as important as what Pam experienced. Her little thirty-second drawing exercise helped her to see her situation differently, and this new perspective helped her to shift gears mentally. Pam quickly saw that she needed to make a change in the way she was approaching the situation. Focusing on the emotional solution is very different from focusing on the problem and trying to intellectually fix it. No one told Pam what to think or believe or do; the new understanding came from within her, through her own hands.

Your own inner wisdom will convince and inspire you far more than any words coming from someone else, no matter how wise or important you think the person is. Your feelings are vitally important, running like an underground river through every part of your life. Conflicted and painful feelings indicate deep hurts that must be drawn out and lovingly tended and integrated into your daily life, or they can be very damaging. You have to find safe ways to be honest with your feelings. Remember, love runs deeper than hurt.

When you are unhappy and feeling uptight, anxious, fearful, angry, distressed, turn within to your heart's inner wisdom. Let

Problems regarding the self, the very personality, can be dealt with by means of visual thought.

• • • Rudolf Arnheim

Inner child exercise (Babs), pencil, 2001

Dancing old woman, ink, 2000

When the drawing was finished the original anger had all vanished. The anger had apparently gone into the drawing.

• • • Joanna Field,
On Not Being Able to Paint

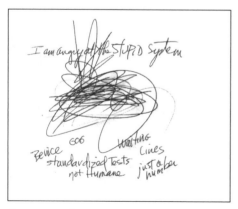

Anger exercise, crayon, 2000

these playful, childlike nondominant-hand drawing exercises help you to focus on the unconditional love that lives beneath the hurt and fear of every situation. See for yourself how close at hand the answer is!

who needs to draw out their feelings?

You are blessed with feelings. Rather than stuffing them down inside or denying that you have them and later exploding in rage — honor your feelings by drawing them out of you in a safe, meaningful, and playful way.

Every human being has feelings. Adults and children all over the world, including Americans, Chinese, Africans, Norwegians, Italians, Mexicans, and Australians, to name just a few of the hundreds of cultures that live on planet earth, have feelings that guide their behavior every day of their lives.

People in different cultures express feelings differently. Asian people can be more reserved. Italians are often more outwardly expressive. Some individuals are more outgoing and emotionally expressive. We call them extroverts. Some people hold their emotions closer to themselves. We call them introverts. All people are a balance of both qualities. There is no right or wrong. Each person is doing the best they can with the knowledge and understanding they have of themselves and the world in which they live.

Sometimes when feelings are expressed, people get hurt. For this reason most cultures have rules about when and how to express feelings. Yet few societies actually teach people how to relieve themselves of painful emotions, like anger, in socially acceptable ways. Just don't let it out is the usual rule. The anger gets stuffed down inside the person. This stuffing hurts the person, maybe not right away, but months or years later.

Families have unwritten rules about expressing emotions. In some families one member always blows up, while the other family members tremble in fear. Some families have an unwritten rule about stuffing their feelings and maintaining a calm outward appearance. Despite inevitable problems, every family is doing the best it can with the knowledge and understanding it has.

It would be very helpful for a family to agree on a safe way to honor and express feelings so that no one gets hurt. It would be helpful for neighborhoods, states, and the nation to do the same.

You are the only person who can explore the vast reaches of your thoughts, feelings, memories, and dreams. You are the only person who can make the necessary changes. Therapeutic, playful, serious, and simple, the drawing exercises I present next will help you express your feelings in a socially acceptable way. This is powerful work — honoring your feelings.

As you move beyond old hurts, new insights come into view. Feelings of love and understanding grow again in your relationships. It is awesome to watch the insights come through your own hands! Who needs to draw out their feelings? Everyone interested in breathing fresh air, emotionally speaking, needs

Detail of drawing on page 94

People enjoy drawing simply because it taps into a universal need to express oneself.

• • • Elizabeth Kübler-Ross, foreword to *The Secret World of Drawing*

Divine quickening, ink, 2000

to. Feelings are an important part of art. And the most important art of all is the art of living.

We all have to learn to honor our feelings in a safe, socially acceptable way. Especially we have to learn *how to learn* from our painful feelings. The drawing exercises in section two of this book are designed to help you do this. I remember a time in my own personal self discovery when an important relationship was breaking up. I was crying while driving at night through the city. To prevent an accident, I pulled over to a safe area, closed the windows, locked the doors, turned off the engine, and honored my feelings by screaming our my pain. When the energy in the feeling was spent, I opened my heart to the lesson in this situation. With a tiny glimpse of that lesson, I was able to let go of my pattern of indentifying myself as a helpless victim and to begin the healthy process of reidentifying myself as consciousness, or mind unfolding — a student of life. I felt lighter and freer as if something significant had shifted in me. Rather than stuffing my feelings, I integrated them.

Bird sitting on woman's finger, ink, 2000

creating a safe environment

Although a safe environment means different things to different people, all people agree that in a safe environment you can sit quietly, breathe deeply, and relax.

If you feel at home in a comfortable room with privacy, you might want to play soothing music, soften the lights, or burn sage, a candle, or incense. Do whatever helps you to relax and focus your attention. Ask housemates and family to respect your need for quiet and privacy while you do this work.

If you are at work and it is too noisy or busy at your desk, you may want to excuse yourself for five minutes. Go to the bathroom or find a place in the building where you can sit alone for a few minutes. If you are in your car waiting for your child at school or at the airport waiting for your flight, instead of just sitting there, take out a piece of paper and draw out your feelings.

Your inner environment is very important. We have all grown up with the belief that some degree of criticism and judgment is necessary to improve our behavior, to get us in line, to make us perfect. The truth is that no one is perfect, and perfection is not the goal of life.

The goal of the following drawing exercises is to help you make friends with yourself. Remember that friendship is based on love, understanding, acceptance, and approval. The goal is also to create a safe environment within you mentally and emotionally so that wherever you go you can be yourself. Everyone around you benefits when you love and accept yourself. Make it okay for you to test things out, to make mistakes, to learn, to feel your feelings, to praise yourself, to laugh and play, to do nothing at all but look at things differently.

unconditional love is available

Sentimental love is expressed only under certain conditions, such as when you clean your room, obey your mate, win the lottery, and so on. It is like the tides, always coming and going.

Unconditional love is very different. It is steady and constant and available to you any time of the day or night, no matter what. You will find that unconditional love is exactly what you need when you work with your emotional feelings. It is very strong and also very tender — protecting you while you explore painful, difficult feelings.

No matter what you are feeling at any given moment, a deeper aspect of your being is not caught up in all the changes, all the moods, all the drama of your life. This deeper part of you is totally worthy of love no matter what you have done. This deeper part of you is totally capable of giving love regardless of your age, height, weight, financial standing, educational status, or reputation in the community.

You are not a limited thing. You are mind unfolding, with the capacity to think and govern thought. You are an energy converter, an individuation of One Infinite Mind. You are the only one who can sort things out in ways that make sense to you. Therapists, teachers, parents, loved ones, gurus, authors, and wise ones are here to help you, but you must do the work.

This work is not difficult. Most of the following drawing exercises require only five to ten minutes of your time to be effective. Please do not labor and sweat over them. Focus your attention, open your heart, listen to the message, and get on with your life in a slightly altered consciousness. Many times this is all you need to breathe fresh air.

Woman planting seeds, ink, 2000

DRAWING EXERCISES

the inner child character

Sometimes we have to work with a memory from childhood, consciously exploring a feeling or an experience of something that happened long ago. When we bring something from the past into the present, we become conscious of an aspect of our unconscious mind. We cannot change the past, but we can bring it into the present moment, where it is possible to change the way we view things. This little shift can be tremendously freeing.

More and more people accept that we all have an inner child and that this special character can help you open the doorway to your interior landscape.

Children approach drawing as play. They have not yet learned rigid rules and regulations about life. They don't know anything about art. All they know is that it feels good to put their feelings and thoughts onto a piece of paper with crayons and pencils. Make your mark! A child confirms his or her existence in many ways: crying out when in pain, laughing, burping, excreting. Drawing can be a fun way for a child to show the world that he or she has a point of view. It is a powerful way to express feelings and to get approval and acceptance.

At some point the child hears that the drawing is wrong: Mommy doesn't like that! Or trees are green, not pink! The child takes the comment personally. Most people stop drawing around the age of nine or ten. Why is this? Around this age children are expected to see things as adults see them; however, they do

Children observe with an acuteness that puts many adults to shame.

• • • Rudolf Arnheim,
Art and Visual Perception

Child playing hide-and-seek, ink, 2000

Except ye become as little children, ye shall not enter into the kingdom of heaven.

• • • Matthew 18:3

Inner child exercise (Sue), crayon, 2000

Inner child exercise (Sue), crayon, 2000

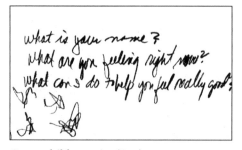

Inner child exercise (Sue), crayon, 2000

not. When their drawings are ridiculed, children come to believe that something is wrong with them. They not only stop drawing, they harbor a secret feeling that something inside them is wrong or not good enough.

This drawing exercise will rekindle a loving, conscious connection with your inner child, no matter how old you are. Together, the two of you can work through this false image of something being wrong with you. Together, the two of you can draw out the deeper truth of your being: You are mind unfolding.

Feelings can help you fulfill your creative potential as an adult. The child part of you will lead the way, doing the drawing in these exercises. Your adult self can relax and watch.

EXERCISE:
Drawing with Your Inner Child

How often can you do this exercise? As often as you feel the desire and need to free yourself to live with new thoughts, new views, new patterns. Louise Hay once asked me to open one of her ten-day intensive trainings by presenting this drawing exercise. I was scared and excited and determined to do an excellent job. I did the inner child exercise (with the three questions) every morning for three months before I went to work. This activity connected me at a very deep level with my own inner child. I recommend that everyone do this exercise every morning or evening for at least thirty days.

1. Relax and breathe. Sit comfortably with paper and crayons before you.
2. Close your eyes for a moment and see or feel a child near you. Notice the color of her hair, her height, her posture and clothing. Open your heart and feel yourself unconditionally accepting this child exactly as she is, even if she is angry, sad, or frightened.
3. Ask this child to play a game with you. Sit down together on the ground or floor of your imagination. The adult you will ask the child you three questions. What is your name? What are you feeling right now? What can I do to help you feel really good?
4. Let the child draw a picture for you using crayons and your nondominant hand.
5. Thank the child for sharing with you.

The creative urge in us is the connecting link that can restore us to the wholeness we have lost. The medicine is already within.

• • • Jan Valentin Saether

the mother character

Everyone has feelings about his or her mother. It does not matter if your mother is (or was) the greatest mother or the worst; eventually you must deal with her. It may not be possible or appropriate for you to talk directly with her, but it is always possible and appropriate for you to work with the images of mother that you carry in your mind and heart every moment of every day.

In this drawing exercise you will have the opportunity to explore a particular memory or feeling attached to the thought of your mother. Remember that you are working with your thoughts, feelings, and memories of your mother, never with the actual person.

Mother and two daughters, ink, 1999

Words softly spoken
Silent thoughts expressed by face and
*   hands.*
Deep emotions stirred from the continent
inside of mind and not of lands
Flowing to the surface into creative art
of many brightly coloured strands.
Revelation.

• • • Mary-Christine

Woman in hot tub being served fruit,
ink, 1999

Perhaps your mother did not provide the kind of love you feel you needed when you were just a child. You may be angry with her. Use this exercise to work through this anger so that you can move forward in your life. Perhaps your mother left you or is not there for you in some way. Use this exercise to work through feelings of abandonment, grief, and sadness that may be holding you back in life.

It is safe and necessary for you to draw out your feelings, whatever they may be. Drawing helps make the process playful, honest, and childlike. In this exercise, on your paper you may tell your mother things you would never say to her in person or write to her in a letter. This frees you and allows you to be honest in ways you could not be while standing face-to-face.

Blaming your mom is not helping her, and it certainly is not helping you. Aim to honestly explore your thoughts and feelings about her. If necessary, be willing to make changes. You do not have to know how — just be willing. Eventually you will come to see that despite her flaws and mistakes, she was doing the best she could with the knowledge and understanding she had at the time. When you understand this, you open the door to forgiveness and to freedom.

Your piece of paper becomes a sacred space in which you can conceive a new image of your mother. It is natural for your understanding to grow; thus it is natural for your new image of your mother to be a little bit more principled, a little more loving, a little more aligned with universal characteristics (unconditional love and acceptance, recognition of your talents and abilities, and so on). The new image of your mother, fashioned by you in your unique way, will open the door to your accepting yourself as a worthy, lovable, bright, capable person. Give yourself now what you needed as a child but for whatever reason did not receive.

Whether or not you have children, you are here to give birth to something very special and totally unique. You need unconditional love and mothering to fulfill your purpose in life.

Our old images can block our fulfillment until either we consciously dissolve them or we in some way see them with greater understanding. Sometimes an old image of our mom stands in the way of our being all we can be. Sometimes we are afraid of displeasing our mother. Feelings about mothers run very deep. Each mother and child has its own issues. Your brother and sister have their own feelings about your mother. Your friends have their own feelings about their mother. Their feelings are not your feelings. Use this opportunity to explore your own feelings about your mother.

I would like to share with you a personal story about my mother's recovery from a massive and unexpected heart attack. My experience, of sitting by her bed and drawing, propelled me into a very deep interior space and led to the writing of this book.

my mother the mermaid

On January 8, 1999, I got two phone messages from my niece, who had called to tell me that my mother had a sudden and completely unexpected massive heart attack. I arranged a flight that night and arrived in Wisconsin the

The capacity to see — to open up the vision of reality that an artist offers, is innate in all of us. I look forward to the day when it will dawn on everybody that they too can have odysseys and Grand Tours and they too can share the fruits of the world.

• • • Sister Wendy Beckett,
Sister Wendy's Grand Tour

My mother the mermaid, ink, 1999

Many artists view art as serious psychological inquiry.

••• Shaun McNiff, *Art As Medicine*

next morning. My sister and I headed straight to the hospital and to the intensive care unit, where Mom was hooked up to many machines, barely conscious, unable to say or do anything. My job was to be there, of that I was sure. I spent three weeks every day at my mother's side, holding her hand, praying and drawing with my nondominant hand. There was nothing else to do.

Each drawing took hours and became a kind of wordless, unconscious dialogue weaving my feelings and thoughts into this incomprehensible experience. While monitors and machines breathed air for Mom and pumped blood for her deeply traumatized heart, I drew. My sister and her two children, the doctors and nurses came and went. Through it all, I drew.

Before this, drawing with my other (my nondominant) hand was an exercise that helped me get around the fast judgments of the intellect. For years I've been using my other hand to follow intuitive hunches and access inner wisdom. I have been teaching this technique since 1987.

This expanse of time, with nothing to do but sit and be there for my mom, gave me a unique opportunity to explore drawing in much greater depth than ever before. I entered a vast new area in consciousness. I did not know what was going to happen to Mom: Would she live or die? I did not know what was going to happen on my paper either. I was in a gentle state of surprise quite a bit of the time.

The mermaid drawing on page 107 and 165 told me that Mother was swimming in very deep water. I knew this, but seeing it on paper helped me accept it.

An ocean liner moves through the night at the top of the drawing. Below the surface are many fish, most of which have large lips. Long ago, my mother confided how embarrassed she was by her large lips. I devoted myself to making big lips on everything, showing the shame that it had nowhere to hide.

In the lower righthand corner sits a snail. At the center of the snail's shell is a face. Before it was a snail shell it was a kind of spidery character with long skinny arms extending in all directions. I felt uncomfortable looking at this character. To me, it represented my mother's heart grasping and struggling to live. It was also my heart struggling to embrace the situation. Although I felt very uneasy looking at this part of the drawing, I did not stop drawing or erase or draw over this corner. I drew in another section of the paper, trusting that later it would become clear to me what I was to do.

At some point I felt comfortable drawing over the spidery arms. That's when I discovered a new character with a new message. The spider became a snail, and the snail told me, *The healing of this situation will take time — be patient.* This made sense to me.

When you draw with your nondominant hand, you discover much about yourself and your world. Don't be too quick to decide what this or that part of your drawing is. Practice being okay with not knowing where the picture is headed. Practice being content letting your heart (the wise advisor) guide you.

I have been drawing all my life and have

Approval and acceptance of the deeper Self makes it possible to receive bravely the real nature of the world.

• • • Abraham Maslow

Detail of drawing on page 107

I believe that we have got to shift our identity out of that little prison cage of ego in order to survive. We have to find ways to know experientially our interconnections with all forms of life on this planet. We need meditations and games and rituals that will give us space to step outside of the human identification we've been wearing for so long.

• • • Joanna Macy

Girl turning back the butterflies, ink, 1999

probably invested more than twenty thousand hours in drawing the human form. What an innocent and powerful way to express emotion. My unconscious mind is filled with visual information about where to put elbows, hands, eyelids, and bellies. Be gentle with yourself while you draw; your drawings will not look like mine, and that is natural and normal.

If you stopped drawing at age nine or so, your drawings will reflect a child's level of seeing, which is perfectly okay for these exercises. Right now, neither of us needs to be concerned with galleries or museums. It is your heart and feelings that you are focusing on. This is not the time to compare yourself with others.

Drawing and writing are some of the ways I use to move through challenges with my heart open — not running away or going into hypervigilant, anxious control. Not knowing whether my mother was going to live or die was a very strange and challenging place. The drawing at the left began when it looked like Mom was going to die. By this time she had been in intensive care for nearly two weeks. The pulmonary specialist said that her heart was not gaining strength and that her breathing was still labored. He mentioned a ventilator — a breathing machine.

The butterflies in the drawing represent transformation. The greatest transformation of all is death. The girl just stands there helpless, facing the advancing ball of butterflies. Her arms hung down limply.

My sister and I sat at a table in the intensive care unit with nine nurses and doctors. We stated Mom's wish not to have extraordinary measures taken to keep her alive, which means no ventilator. A no-code bracelet was put on mom's arm stating that she was not to be revived if she slipped toward death.

Almost immediately, I believe it was the next day, Mom's strength began to return. Slowly the hospital staff took her off some of the machines. One week later she was sitting up in a chair next to the bed eating pudding.

At some point I drew the girl's arms facing up, palms out, as if the girl was saying, *I am not ready just yet.*

I remember sitting next to Mom's chair and showing her these drawings. She was filled with gratitude and a lovely softness. All she said was, "They are beautiful."

This drawing emerged after two or three days of scribbling and scratching. I was amazed as this strong, young woman appeared. Above her the sky was full of hearts, and the ground was soaked with blood. Her traumatic experience had cut her to the core, yet these hearts were singing a rousing song. It made me wonder if there wasn't something positive behind all this pain.

The naked girl told me that a vulnerable strength was developing. Mom was still in the intensive care unit — anything could happen. Hands open outward as if she were bringing forward something from her heart. Is my mother bringing something forward from her heart? What is it?

I recalled visiting Mom three months before the heart attack. We were sitting in the living room when she said, "Oh, I have so many regrets!" I remember thinking, "I'm not going to feed into this by commenting or

It takes courage to follow your own course, beyond the expectations of parents, friends, and institutions.

• • • Marsha Sinetar

Girl bringing something forward from
her heart, ink, 1999

I have lived far away from my mother for most of my adult life. I visit her about every two years or so. On one visit in 1984, I asked Mom to sit in her favorite chair — I wanted to draw her. She sat almost perfectly still for two hours, and we hardly spoke.

My mother, graphite, 1984

defending myself." Outwardly I let it pass, but inwardly an old resistance flooded up through my veins: I was sure she was referring to me.

I know I have not turned out as she had hoped. I resisted traditional education, barely graduating from college. I moved to San Francisco, was a hippie in the latter part of the 1960s, a spiritual searcher in the '70s, an artist's apprentice in the '80s, an artist and teacher in the '90s. I knew early on that I would not have kids, that this lifetime was an opportunity for me to learn how to move beyond the patterns of my past. Mom, a very traditional and conservative lady, was not impressed.

However, I realized that I did not need to take her statement personally. In fact, I may not have been the source of her regrets.

About six months after the heart attack, I returned for a one-week visit. It was clear that she was recovering. One day I quietly asked if she remembered saying that she had many regrets. It seemed to be important to me to gently explore with her the connection between her emotions, thoughts, and body. After all, her heart was functioning at only 11 percent of its capacity; she needed all the help she could get, and we both knew that drugs couldn't do it all.

Yes, she remembered saying that.

She agreed that it is possible that her regrets may have contributed in some way to her heart attack. Her heart did not attack her — the regrets may have done the job! Very clearly and slowly, she said these words: "I'm not going to do that anymore!" Huge chunks of emotional debris dissolve and float away from the walls of your veins and arteries when you decide to let go of old regrets.

Today, at age ninety, nearly three years after the heart attack, Mom lives alone, cooks her meals, washes her dishes, makes her bed, watches the news, and goes to church on Sunday. She naps the rest of the day. She takes many different drugs, has a defibrulator in her chest, and has no time for painful emotions, regrets, criticisms, or judgments.

Now it is time to focus on your mother. It does not matter if she is alive or if she has passed on. It does not matter if she is your blood mother, your adopted mother, or your foster mother. You have an image of mother inside you — and lots of feelings. This is where you work. Even an image of emptiness is an image.

Be prepared to see your mother differently. You may even come to see yourself differently.

Change is natural and normal as you grow and unfold a greater understanding of yourself, of your parents, and of others. Give yourself lots of love during this process. You need your own love and acceptance in order to fulfill the unique purpose that you were born to express.

The mother character is central to your life in many ways. Following are two exercises to help you draw out your feelings about your mother. The Dialogue with Your Mother exercise is a simple dialogue with words. The Drawing Your Mother exercise begins with a drawing and includes a dialogue. Use crayons — and both hands. Your adult self uses your dominant hand. Your mother uses your nondominant hand, telling you how she feels.

Art and art only can cause violence to be set aside.

• • • Leo Tolstoy

Education through art is education for peace.

• • • Sir Herbert Read

Mother and daughter with stars, ink, 1999

No one can get anywhere without contemplation.

• • • Robert Henri, *The Art Spirit*

This is a focused imaginative dialogue that flows between you and mother. Both exercises can be done once or many times. Use my exercises as they are and make up your own versions as you go along. Play gentle instrumental music and take as long as you wish. Have Kleenex nearby, since these exercises can be emotional.

The greatest joy for a child is to please its mother. The greatest joy for an adult is to live in accordance with his or her life purpose. Each child's path is different. Sometimes you can't please your mother and also live your purpose. Love and forgiveness is required here.

Mama, I love you forever, ink, 2000

EXERCISE:
Dialogue with Your Mother

Have a dialogue with your mother using both hands. Your dominant hand expresses your point of view. Your other hand expresses your mother's point of view. You can do this if you are on good speaking terms or not, whether your mother is alive or dead. Don't think about these issues or worry about doing it right. Open your heart to your feelings. Allow a deeper part of yourself to imagine what your mother's feelings are. Just relax and allow feelings to flow onto the paper.

1. Tell your mother honestly and exactly how you feel. She then tells you how she feels.
2. Tell your mother what you needed to hear from her when you were a child. She then

tells you what she needed to hear from her mother when she was a child.

3. Tell your mother what you really love in life and what your dreams are. She then tells you what she really loves in life and what her dreams are.

 Close by thanking your mother and yourself for sharing.

EXERCISE:
Drawing Your Mother

1. Sit and breathe. Imagine your mother standing before you. How do you feel?

2. With pen, pencil, or crayons, draw an outline of her body on your paper using your nondominant hand.

3. Did she at some point experience a jolt (heart attack, cancer, divorce, death of a loved one) of some kind?

4. Using your nondominant hand, draw a mark on her body to represent this jolt.

5. With your dominant hand, write on your paper: Jolt, tell me about yourself.
Write the answer with your other hand.

6. With your dominant hand, write: Jolt, where in my own life are you expressing yourself?
Write the answer with your other hand.

7. With your dominant hand, write: Mother, thank you for being the vehicle for my life here on earth. Wherever you are right now, I free you to go and be and do what pleases you. And I free myself to do the same. Mother, is there something I can do to help you feel really good?

Mother exercise (Sue), graphite, 2000

This drawing of my dad is special to me because it was done just two weeks before he died. Here he was, sitting at the kitchen table in my sister's house, looking around for someone to talk with. Dad was a philosopher and long-standing member of the Socialist Labor Party, and he believed that people were to help one another, care for one another, and work together to share the wealth and prosperity of this great earth. Greed, competition, and war were the result of ignorance. He felt that education was the path to peace.

My father loved to dance to big band music. Many times he and his girlfriend, Dorothy, took me to senior dances around Chicago. One month before he died from lung cancer, he handed me an audiotape he had made of his favorite big band songs. We sat and listened to it for a bit. Then he stood up and offered me his hand, and we danced.

My father, Prismacolor pencil, 1993

8. Write and draw your mother's answer with your nondominant hand.
9. Close by thanking both your mother and yourself for sharing.

the father character

Everyone has feelings about his or her father. It does not matter if your father is (or was) the greatest father or the worst; eventually you must deal with him.

Resolving conflicting feelings about your father can be very important. It can often clear up issues with your career, your sense of success or failure, your reputation and standing in the community, your sense of fulfillment.

It may not be possible or appropriate for you to talk directly with your father, but it is always possible and appropriate for you to work with the images of father that you carry in your mind and heart, every moment of every day. The images can change, and when they do, you also change in some way. The image of father in your consciousness, not the actual person, is what you are working with in the following drawing exercises.

Perhaps your father did not provide the kind of support you needed when you were just a child. You may be angry with him. Use the next exercise to work through this anger so that you can move forward in your life. Perhaps your father left you or is not there for you in some way. Use this exercise to work through feelings of abandonment, grief, and sadness that may be holding you back in life.

Perhaps there was abuse. If so, it may be best to do these exercises with a professional counselor or therapist. A drawing can be worth a thousand words — very helpful in a therapeutic relationship. Notice your feelings. If you feel sad for several days after doing this exercise, remember that reaching out to ask for help is a measure of your strength.

Drawing your feelings onto paper with your nondominant hand is one of the safest and most powerful ways to express your feelings. Drawing makes the process playful, honest, and relevant. On paper you can tell your father things you would never say to him in person or write to him in a letter.

I loved my father, but like many fathers, he was not around much. I did not learn how to set boundaries, aim for goals, or manage a career.

When I began my apprenticeship with master painter Jan Valentin Saether, I was thirty-four years old. I had doubts about what I was doing with my life. Other people had careers, families, big incomes, and here I was — still yearning to learn, to follow my heart, and to trust my creativity. I knew Mr. Saether could teach me something I would *never* get in a university. I did not really feel ready to teach art. There was something more to experience. But was this the right course for me to follow?

I decided to talk to myself as if I were a good father giving me fatherly advice. *Draw and paint with Mr. Saether for two years. If you produce two works that demonstrate high quality, I will allow you to continue. Otherwise you will have to stop focusing on art and devote yourself to some career that is more practical.*

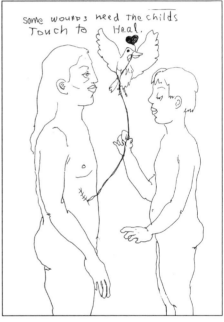

Child healing the adult, ink, 1999

Discover where your personal story joins a universal story. Find broader contexts and richer, wiser formulations, with more abundant cues and patterns on which to draw and from which to redirect your life.

• • • Jean Houston,
The Search for the Beloved

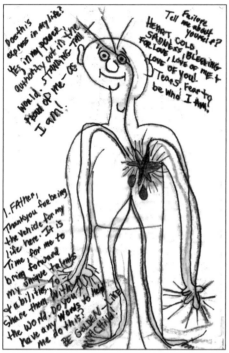

Father exercise (Cindy), crayon and marker, 2001

This father-daughter talk with myself really helped. It gave me exactly what I needed: a clear boundary and a goal I loved. Many times I almost quit during the first two years of the apprenticeship, yet my clear, loving fatherly advice to myself kept me going. Basically, I fathered myself. Perhaps your father influenced a different aspect of your life.

Everyone has an imperfect human father, and everyone also has a perfect father principle. When the human father fails you, the image of your perfect father is ready, willing, and able to be born in you. Your consciousness and your piece of paper are wonderful places to conceive a new and more principled image of your father.

Feelings about our fathers run very deep. Use this opportunity to explore your feelings about your father.

EXERCISE:
Dialogue with Your Father

Adapt this exercise to help you work through patterns in your life that may involve your father. Have a dialogue with your father using both hands. Your dominant hand expresses your point of view. Your other hand expresses your father's point of view. You can do this whether or not you are on good speaking terms, whether your father is alive or dead. Don't think about these issues or worry about doing it right. Open your heart to your feelings. Allow a deeper part of yourself to imagine your father's feelings. Just relax and allow feelings to flow onto the paper.

1. Tell your father honestly and completely exactly how you feel. He then tells you how he feels.
2. Tell him what you needed to hear from him when you were a child. He then tells you what he needed to hear from his father when he was a child.
3. Tell him what you really love in life and what your dreams are. He then tells you what he really loves in life and what his dreams are.

   Close by thanking your father and yourself for sharing.

EXERCISE:
Drawing Your Father

Adapt this exercise to help you work through patterns in your life that may involve your father.

1. Sit and breathe. Contemplate your father for one minute, silently.
2. Using your nondominant hand, draw an outline of your father's body.
3. Ask yourself where in his life your father failed. What was the nature of this failure? Did his body — stomach, heart, kidneys, lungs — fail? Did he fail financially? Creatively?
4. With pen, pencil, or crayons, draw a mark or marks somewhere on his body to represent this failure.

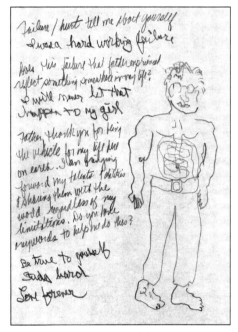

Father exercise (Cindy), graphite, 2001

5. With your dominant hand, write: Failure, tell me about yourself. Write the answer with your nondominant hand.

6. With your dominant hand, write: Does this failure express itself anywhere in my life? If so, where? Write the answer with your nondominant hand.

7. With your dominant hand, write: Father, thank you for being the vehicle for my life here on earth. It is time for me to bring forward my unique talents and abilities, to share them with the world. Do you have any words to help me do this?

8. Write and draw your father's answer with your nondominant hand.

9. Close by thanking yourself and your father for sharing.

My friends from Ireland, ink, 2000

reparenting

In ancient Hawaii, children were raised by the entire community. When a baby was born, an elder woman was given the duty of watching it. This woman was no ordinary baby-sitter. The old woman observed many characteristics of the child: his sensitivity to color and sound, slow or quick movements of the hands and legs, the way he played with toys, other children, and natural objects.

After about a year, the old woman told the child's parents who in the community shared a similar temperament with this child. The parents made sure that the child and this similar person spent time together. Being near someone who is like you in temperament helps you to feel seen. To express yourself creatively you need to feel seen by someone.

Some parents may not appreciate their child's temperament. Children, then, have to find their own ways to be seen and appreciated for who they are. If for any reason you feel that you were not seen as a child or that you are not appreciated as an adult, this exercise will help you open your heart to see yourself through the Divine Mother Principle and the Divine Father Principle.

Reparenting yourself is a bit like being reborn. You realign or reidentify yourself with the formless principles of mothering and fathering. Principles are the source of every physical form. They are like God: They are everywhere evenly present and invisible, operating behind the scenes. Here are a few principles that though they are at work every day, we seldom think about: (1) the principle of flight, (2) the principle of gravity, (3) the principle of electricity, and (4) the principle of locomotion.

Reparenting exercise, ink, 2000

Reparenting exercise, ink, 2000

EXERCISE:
Reparenting Yourself

1. Sit, breathe, and relax your tummy, jaw, and wrist.
2. Bring to mind your mother and father (biological, adoptive, or foster, living or dead). See them before you at a little distance. Notice their posture and expressions.
3. With your nondominant hand, draw a simple outline of your mother and father. You may use crayons, pencil, or pen.

4. Behind your mother is the Divine Mother Principle. Behind your father is the Divine Father Principle.
5. Draw shapes to express these principles.
6. Ask these parenting principles to tell you about yourself. Ask the Mother Principle: What qualities do you see in me? Ask the Father Principle: What qualities do you see in me?
7. Draw or write further as you wish. Different qualities will come up at different times to help you with specific situations.
8. Thank the Divine Mother and Father Principles for sharing with you. Return as often as you wish for further guidance and instruction.
9. Give a title or name to your drawing. If you have time, write about how you feel having your qualities and characteristics seen.

self-acceptance

Making friends with yourself is the first step in creating top-quality experiences and in exploring the dynamic connection between thoughts and circumstances. One of the first qualities that defines a good friend is that he or she accepts you exactly as you are.

Many people are confused. Some believe they cannot accept themselves because they are sinful. Others believe they have to be perfect before they can accept themselves. Still others have come to the point of accepting themselves intellectually but cannot really accept themselves in their hearts. All people are somewhere

The creator made us creative. Our creativity is our gift from God. Our use of it is our gift to God. Accepting this bargain is the beginning of true self-acceptance.

• • • Julia Cameron, *The Artist's Way*

Woman talking into the mirror, ink, 2000

in the process of learning how to open their hearts, to love and accept themselves unconditionally, exactly as they are. Self-acceptance is one of the biggest lessons in life.

The problem is that we are conditioned to judge, analyze, and criticize ourselves to determine whether or not we are worthy of acceptance. If we win the race, the applause, the lottery, the position, we feel worthy. We feel unworthy if we lose.

The solution is close at hand. Self-acceptance can be achieved very simply and easily by opening your heart and choosing to love and accept yourself exactly as you are right now — no matter what is going on, who you are with, what grade you got, how you feel, or what someone else is doing.

Stop the chattering mind.

Drop into your heart space.

Accept yourself exactly as you are.

Look into a mirror, into your eyes, and say the following words sincerely to yourself, to the being that lives inside you. Say them simply, directly, and with feeling: I love and approve of you.

Self-acceptance exercise, first part, ink, 2001

EXERCISE: Self-Acceptance

1. Sit and breathe. Relax your shoulders, tummy, and jaw.
2. Choose a problem or issue. With your nondominant hand, write the problem on your paper. Use crayons, pastels, pen, or pencil.
3. Draw marks to express your feelings about this problem.

Self-acceptance exercise, second part, ink, 2001

4. Place this problem into your heart and feel your heart accept it exactly as it is. Notice what it feels like to accept a problem exactly as it is.
5. Ask: What do I need to know about this?
6. Just listen.
7. Draw or write marks to express what your heart tells you.
8. Write on your paper with your nondominant hand: I accept myself exactly as I am.
9. Write on your paper any feelings that come up in response to this statement.

It is said that the Buddha once gave a sermon without saying a word; he merely held up a flower to his listeners. This was the famous flower sermon — a sermon in the language of patterns, the silent language of flowers.

• • • Gyorgy Doczi, *The Power of Limits*

Watching the sun set, ink, 2001

being alone

Believe it or not, being alone is a sacred experience. When you are alone (all-one), you can hear your own thoughts and feel your own feelings. You can hear the still, small voice, guiding and directing your behavior from deep within you.

Alone time is a good time to make friends with yourself. When you are on friendly terms with yourself — loving and accepting yourself unconditionally — you find peace and joy and balance and harmony within. Even when the world outside is crashing down around you, on the inside you know you are loved and worthy.

When you are not on friendly terms with yourself, you find judgments, harsh critical words, and even feelings of self-hatred. Life is very hard when you hate yourself and feel you are not good enough. You cannot change others, but you can change your own negative thoughts and feelings.

Society conditions us to be social, popular, part of the crowd. When we see people who are alone, we feel sorry for them or frightened of them as if there were something wrong with them. However, all leaders, artists, inventors, and true individuals value alone time. If you want to bring something new into the world, you have to learn how to enjoy and value being alone.

Strengthen your relationship with yourself by practicing this drawing exercise.

The real issue is not the fear but how we hold the fear.

• • • Susan Jeffers,
Feel the Fear and Do It Anyway

EXERCISE: Being Alone

1. Sit alone, breathe, and relax.
2. What does being alone feel like to you in the present moment?
3. Using crayons and your nondominant hand, draw marks that express your feelings about being alone. Accept your feelings.
4. Ask your heart: What do I need to know about being alone? Listen to what it says.
5. Draw or write what it says.

anxiety

The emotional atmosphere of the home where you grew up teaches you at a deep unconscious level how to handle your feelings. Some people hold feelings in, while others spew them out. You learn from the adults around you. If your father tightened his gut to hold his feelings in, you may do the same without even knowing it. If your mother was overwhelmed a lot and cried to get attention, you may do the same with your partner. Emotional patterns run

Man and his teddy, ink, 2000

Accuse exercise (Sue), ink, 2001

Accuse exercise, ink, 2002

deep. Still, with awareness, love, and acceptance of yourself, you can change these patterns.

Millions of people suffer from varying degrees of anxiety, taking drugs to get relief from anxious thoughts, panic attacks, excess nervous energy, and physical effects such as high blood pressure. This drawing exercise is not meant to replace therapy or drugs. It is to help you do some safe exploring on your own or with your doctor. Many therapists employ drawing as a beneficial aid in the therapeutic process.

> ### EXERCISE:
> # Drawing Out Anxiety

1. Sit, breathe, and relax your tummy and jaw.
2. Feel the anxiety in you right now. Where is it: tummy, jaw, legs, head?
3. Using crayons and your nondominant hand, draw this anxiety out of you and put it on your paper. Let it take whatever shape feels right.
4. Ask the anxiety: What do I need to know?
5. Write or make marks that express what it tells you.

accuse and release

Feelings and emotion are like water — they must flow or they stagnate. The trouble is, you can't shout with anger at your boss whenever the feeling comes up. You have to find another way.

This drawing exercise is to be done swiftly,

in the heat of the moment when your feelings are hot, loud, burning inside you. Don't wait to calm down and get reasonable. Honor your feelings exactly as they are, express them in a safe way, and let them go. You may be led to a new mind-set that allows you to see the issue or situation from a whole new angle.

To face injustice, abuse, pain, sorrow, or any other wound in your consciousness would be impossible were it not for the love that is asking to be released from the hurt place. The hurts in life are signals telling us where love is locked up inside us. Love lives beneath anger, fear, hurt, and pain. Love is the solution to every problem. Go for the love as you accuse those who do you wrong. Love heals.

The person who wronged you is not to be part of this exercise; it is your thoughts of the person that you speak to. Say the name of the person and see him or her in your mind's eye. Tell this person exactly how you feel and what he or she did to you. Accuse yourself for getting into the situation in the first place. Exhaust yourself with accusations, and when there is no more to say, shift gears and move into releasing.

It takes two to tango. Even if one person appears to be at fault, everyone involved played a part. Everyone has something to learn. Accuse and Release is a healthy way to honor your feelings and return to love. The lesson is always love: of yourself, of life, of another. Einstein said it well: "The solution and the problem are two different mind-sets. To heal your life, you must change your mind."

Accuse exercise (Kathy), ink, 2002

Whether the shadow becomes your friend or enemy depends largely upon ourselves. The shadow is like any human being with whom one has to get along, sometimes by giving in, sometimes by resisting, sometimes by giving love, whatever the situation requires. The shadow becomes hostile only when he is ignored or misunderstood.

• • • M. L. von Franz

Refreshing release, ink, 2000

EXERCISE: Accuse and Release

1. Sit, breathe, and relax your tummy and jaw. Picture the person you need to accuse. Say her or his name. (If more than one person is to be accused, imagine their coming forward one at a time. If a whole group is involved, accuse the group.)

2. Using crayons and your nondominant hand, draw your accusations. Scribble your feelings. Accuse with present-tense words and feelings. Be angry or sad, swear, shake your fists, cry, sob, yell into a pillow. Be real! State exactly what the person did to hurt you. (For example: You lied to me! You abandoned me!) Empty yourself completely of all accusations until no more come. Turn to yourself and accuse yourself. (For example: I may accuse myself for not speaking my truth, or I may accuse myself of doing exactly what I have just accused the person of doing. I sometimes hurt myself in similar ways, and this person may have just portrayed this pattern of mine for me to see so that I could free myself of it. This realization, by the way, can lead to a full transformation.)

3. Draw the old, limiting identity dissolving. Draw a deeper part of yourself — your true identity as consciousness cleansing you like clean, pure water. Say silently to yourself and to everyone involved in this learning situation: This experience is helping to free me from an old, false identity as a limited being. As I free myself to be who I really am, I also free you to go and be and do whatever pleases you! Thank you.

Be gentle with yourself. Sometimes you can only release a little portion of the love that is locked inside the pain. Accept every effort as good and know that there is more to learn.

safely expressing anger

Anger is normal — everyone feels it now and then. Expressing anger safely is important for all of us. Stuffing it or making yourself wrong for feeling angry forces you to carry it, sometimes for years. Anger, channeled properly, can move you out of stuck places, can motivate you to act, can enforce justice rather than bend to ignorance.

How did your parents and siblings handle anger? Was it volcanic? Did they use the silent treatment? Did everyone yell and scream, or was only one person allowed to do that? How do you deal with anger today? Are you frightened of it?

On a piece of paper you can get as angry as you want and yet no one gets hurt — not even yourself. Drawing is a safe, effective, even enjoyable way to channel your anger. Drawing makes anger visible so you can better understand yourself and the situations you find yourself in.

Drawing is a wonderful way to get rid of anger or whatever you want to get rid of.

• • • Elizabeth Layton, *Women and Aging*

Two angry volcanoes, ink, 1999

EXERCISE:
Drawing Out Your Anger

1. With your nondominant hand, write on the top of your paper, I am angry at _____. Fill in the name or situation.
2. Close your eyes and feel the anger. Notice where it is in your body.

3. Imagine the anger flowing out of you. Draw the anger out of you. Keep drawing until the last bit of it (for now) is on the paper.

4. Listen to yourself as you draw. Notice the words you are using to express this anger. Write them down. You may see a pattern.

5. When you feel there is no more anger in you, step back and breathe.

6. Thank yourself for expressing your anger in this safe way.

7. Give this drawing a title. Show it to your therapist, put it in journal, or burn it in a little ceremony.

forgiveness

Forgiveness means giving up your limited view to gain a greater understanding. It is a gift you give to yourself. Forgiveness frees you from the prison of painful feelings like hurt, anger, resentment, guilt, and fear. Change your consciousness, not the other person. You may say the words *I forgive you,* but if you do not change the pattern in your consciousness that created the situation, you cannot move beyond it.

If someone cuts you off on the freeway, somewhere inside you is a pattern that cuts you off. Perhaps long ago someone cut you off in some way. Or perhaps you cut off other people abruptly and don't know it. Somewhere you are storing pain. Instead of continuing to hold onto it, instead of inflicting your pain on others, forgive them.

Forgiveness exercise, ink, 2000

This drawing exercise is very simple. Name the pattern that is limiting you in some way and draw it out of you. This is easier than it sounds, because the truth of you has never been stuck or caught up in it in the first place.

EXERCISE: Forgiveness

1. Name the limited pattern.
2. Name how you feel about it.
3. Name the person or persons who are caught up in this pattern with you.
4. Name a positive function of this pattern that would benefit you and all involved.
5. Declare: I am willing to change the pattern in my consciousness that creates this condition (whatever it is). I exchange the old identity of myself as a thing that can be hurt for a greater understanding of myself as mind unfolding. I free everyone to go and be and do whatever pleases you. I free myself.
6. Using your nondominant hand and crayons, draw a picture of the new you.

emotional overwhelm

Lola, a savvy corporate executive, came to a women's discussion group frazzled, saying she was overwhelmed emotionally. Four people had caused major upsets in her life the past week, and this put her over the edge. She felt disoriented, unable to feel her soul. Not able to center herself, she did not know what to do.

I knew that if I could get her to focus on these four people, she would find her way back.

Emotional overwhelm exercise (Kathy), ink, 2000

I asked her if she was willing to try a drawing exercise, and she said yes. I don't have Lola's drawings, though I recall them as small, faint pencil marks. They did not look like much, but to Lola they were powerful expressions of her feelings about these four people. The act of drawing the four figures and letting her feelings flow gave her the emotional space she needed to see that she was more in control of things than she had thought.

When emotions are oceanic, we desperately try to figure things out with our intellect. Yet its limited, linear approach just can't always do the job. You feel like you are sinking in this sea of overwhelm. You need to focus your attention with the right brain. Your heart, like your emotions, is oceanic, and it can help you swim to shore. Drawing your heart out onto a piece of paper can help you gain the edge you need to pull yourself out of emotional overwhelm.

EXERCISE: Expressing Emotional Overwhelm

1. Who or what is causing you to feel overwhelmed? Using crayons and your nondominant hand, draw a box for each cause, then title each box.
2. See each person or issue one at a time in your imagination. Make marks expressing your feelings for each in the appropriate box.
3. Acknowledge your feelings. They are no longer inside you; they are right in front of you on your paper. Here you can exert a bit of control (the edge you need).

4. You are more than your feelings. These people, too, are more than what they appear to be. Acknowledge the deeper self in you and in everyone involved.

5. Ask the deeper self in you to make its presence known on your paper.

intimacy and power

Many people believe that you get love and power from your partner. This false belief leads to dysfunction in relationships in which people manipulate and control to get their needs met. You could see this drama enacted every day in television soap operas. But when you get tired of soap operas, you will want to explore real love and intimacy.

Intimate means essential and innermost. An intimate relationship with another person brings you into an intimate relationship with your own essential and innermost self. This relationship empowers you to love yourself and others.

Where do you get love and power? From the essential self within you. The exciting thing is that your partner can help you find this love and power within you. And, furthermore, you can help your partner to find this love and power within her or him.

How it feels to be dependent upon an outside source for love and power.

I am always looking outside myself. I'm never good enough. Other people appear to be better or worse than me.

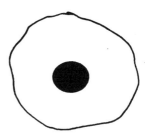

How it feels to be in my power!

Here I am centered and relaxed within myself. No one is on a pedestal. I listen to my heart and have compassion for myself and others.

Intimacy and power exercise, ink, 2000

EXERCISE:
Intimacy and Power

1. Sit, breathe, and relax. Contemplate your intimate relationship with your partner or with someone else, like a sibling or friend.

2. Using crayons and your nondominant hand, draw on the left side of your paper how you feel when you are dependent on your partner (or any outside source) for love and power.

3. Draw on the right side of your paper how you feel when you are in your power, sharing it with love.

4. Contemplate three ways to express your love and power every day. Contemplate three ways to honor your partner's expression of power. Everyone is unique. There is no right or wrong way.

dialogue with another's essential self

Nana Veary, a beloved Hawaiian woman, wrote a wonderful book called *Change We Must* in which she shares her spiritual journey. She says that when you have difficulty with someone, it is very helpful to talk with his or her essential self (the inner advisor) about the issue.

Sometimes it is not possible to talk directly with a person. If you feel you might explode with anger, fall apart in tears, or be manipulated by a loved one if you talk to them face-to-face, this drawing exercise can help provide a connection. If you feel you may not be as strong with a colleague as you need to be, this exercise may strengthen you to say what needs to be said. If you are a teacher searching for the words to inspire your students, it can open the door to your drawing out of them what they yearn to know. If you have something to

Dialogue with another's essential self, ink, 2000

share but they don't listen, speak to their essential self with this drawing exercise.

> ### EXERCISE: Dialogue with Another's Essential Self

1. Sit, breathe, and contemplate the person whose essential self you wish to talk with.
2. Imagine that this person's essential self is before you now. Using crayons and your nondominant hand, write her or his name.
3. Ask: What do I need to know (about you, about myself)? Ask whatever you want to know.
4. Draw a picture with your nondominant hand, or just make marks.
5. Ask the person's essential self to interpret the drawing.
6. Give this drawing a title or name. If you have time, write a story about it.
7. Thank the person's essential self for sharing.

body wisdom

The body is constantly communicating with the mind. Our ancestors long ago in much simpler times knew that the body and mind were one. During the Enlightenment, with the introduction of the scientific inquiry into nature, the body was thought to be separate from the mind and Spirit. Current cutting-edge thinking (quantum physics, for example) is that body and mind are actually expressions of one consciousness. The body is, in a sense, the skin of the mind.

My body really talked to me, not just to tell me what hurt—but why. What I find is that it's never what we think. I would have suspected that my neck is sore because of bending over a desk all day, but my neck told me that "I'm tired, I'm scared"...and I knew just what it meant by that. How wonderful.

• • • Kathy from Canada

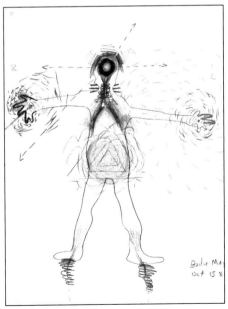

Body wisdom exercise (Allen),
crayons, 1989

While swimming laps one day, in an Olympic-sized pool, I noticed that I felt exhausted after only a few laps. No physical problem was apparent. I realized that my thinking was scattered and unfocused, and I decided to experiment. I swam a lap while focusing on a particular problem I was trying to solve. Almost immediately, it seemed, I reached the other side. I swam another lap, and another! My once tired body transformed when I focused my mind. I concluded that the body follows the mind like a puppy follows its master. We are consciousness first and body second.

On pages 135 through 140 are some actual student responses to my Body Wisdom exercise. This drawing exercise was presented many times at the Louise Hay International Teacher Trainings from 1995 to 2001. The in-sights that more than eight hundred participants gained from this simple drawing exercise were beneficial and helpful to them not only in making changes in the way they lived physically but also in the way they held their emotions and the way they maintained their beliefs about life. When change is needed, it is made much more easily when you can see how you feel about it.

Body Wisdom is a dialogue with the sensations of your body. You do not enter this dialogue to have perfect control over your body; you enter it to learn, to grow, to open your heart, and to be willing to heal, to make changes, to listen, to make friends with your body, and to love it exactly as it is.

As Jan from Greece contemplates changes that are coming in her life, she notices that her heart pounds and her arms tighten. So she has

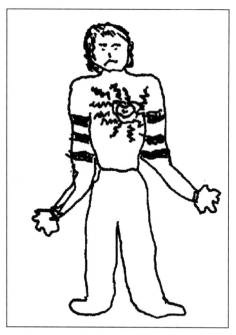

Body wisdom focus on arms A (Jan), ink, 2000

a dialogue with her arms and chest. To the left (page 136) is her first drawing — Drawing A.

Jan: Arms, why do you feel so heavy?

Arms: You don't listen to your heart. You are afraid of change. You want to move forward, but you still listen to the fear. This creates conflict.

Jan: I feel these feelings in my arms when I am trying to figure out what I really want to do. How do I know what I really want when for so long I've done what I've thought others wanted? Arms, why do you squeeze and restrain me?

Arms: I am not doing the restraining — you are. You are reaching out but are using your fear, your excuses, other people's stuff, to hold you back, to restrain you. You are doing it — I'm just helping you to feel it!

Can you see how when Jan listens to her bodily sensations she is able to gain important emotional wisdom? Notice that the armbands, in Drawing B, are a little looser than they are in Drawing A. The thick, heavy armbands in Drawing A have become thin pieces of string in Drawing B. Her heart looks stressed in Drawing A, while in Drawing B it is drawn radiating love. She's opening up!

Jan reports one year later: "I have left Greece, my husband, his paycheck, my family in England, and have found a place to live for six months in Taos, New Mexico, with a magnificent view of the mountain. There is some insecurity, but it is nowhere near what it was this time last year."

Body wisdom focus on arms B (Jan), ink, 2000

Healing is not the same as curing. Healing does not mean going back to the way things were before, but rather allowing "what is now" to move us closer to God.

••• Ram Dass

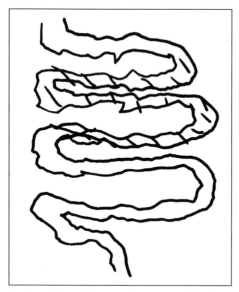

Body wisdom focus on intestines (Linda), ink, 1999

Linda from New England felt tension in the upper part of her intestines. Below is the dialogue she had with her intestines. To the left is her drawing.

Linda: Intestines, why do you feel tense?

Intestines: When you were young you were told that women could be teachers or nurses and then only before or after children. You were also not encouraged to continue your artistic talents. The fear about earning money keeps coming up.

Linda: What can I do to release this tension so that I can feel good about earning money?

Intestines: Oh, that is easy. Use that affirmation about deserving to earn.

Linda: Why is only the upper half of you marked?

Intestines: Other fears pervade that area.

Linda: What more do I need to know about money?

Intestines: You fear that should you earn vast amounts, you won't know how to handle it. Be assured of two things: You will always have it. And you will know how to handle all you have.

Jeni from England, a workshop facilitator, was experiencing a case of nervous energy, fear, and anxiety about an upcoming workshop. She noticed that the back of her throat felt heavy. The throat is responsible for two very important functions. One, your survival depends on your ability to swallow food. Two, a great deal of your individual expression flows through the sound of your voice and words.

Jeni decided to have a dialogue with her throat. To the right is her drawing.

Jeni: What is the purpose of this heaviness?
Throat: I know you can lead the workshop.
Jeni: What is the lump?
Throat: The lump in your throat is there from your childhood when you were given a blockage from your dad. He didn't think you were good enough to stand up in front of people. He was so critical.

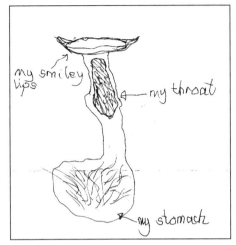

Body wisdom focus on throat (Jeni), graphite, 1998

Karen from England had a dialogue with her throat and asked some similar questions. She, too, is a workshop facilitator, though she is just beginning this career.

Karen: Tight feeling in my throat, please tell me about yourself.
Throat: I'm the little you. I'm tight to stop you from being foolish.
Karen: What can I do to make you feel good and happy?
Throat: Listen to yourself. Support yourself. Be gentle. Stop being little — it serves no one. Be yourself. Be big!

Mary from Australia was asked to consider feeling worthy doing work that she loved. Right away she noticed that she felt a hardening in her hands and chest and throat whenever her thoughts turned to being paid. She feels she doesn't know enough to be well paid. Her drawing is on page 140.

Mary: Hello, tight feeling in my chest, throat, and hands. What is your purpose for

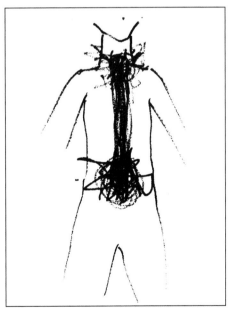

Body wisdom focus on throat (Karen), crayon, 1999

Body wisdom focus on chest and hands
(Mary), crayon, 1998

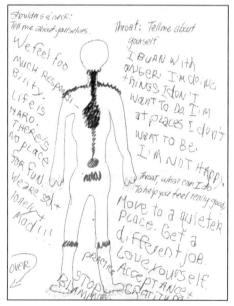

Body wisdom focus on shoulders and
throat (Kathy), crayon, 1997

being in my body at this time? First of all, let's talk to my hands.

Hands: I want to write for you and you keep saying, "Don't write."

Mary: But the thoughts get stuck, and I don't know what to write.

Hands: I think the thoughts do come, but you won't put them down because you are comparing yourself to others.

Mary: This feels true. How can I change this?

Hands: By believing in yourself and your ability.

Mary: I know I am worthy but somehow I forget. Whenever I become aware of this hard feeling in my chest or throat or hands, I will remember to tell myself that I am worthy, that my unique expression is wonderful. I already feel my chest soften and open with these words. Thank you, chest and throat and hands for your helpful wisdom.

Kathy from Vermont felt a burning in her throat and shoulders. On paper she drew heavy lines over those areas.

Kathy: Shoulders, tell me about yourselves.

Shoulders: We feel too much responsibility. Life is hard. There's no place for fun. We are sad and lonely and mad.

Kathy: Throat, tell me about yourself.

Throat: I burn with anger. I'm doing things I don't want to do. I'm at places I don't want to be. I'm not happy.

Kathy: Throat and shoulders, what can I do to help you feel really good?

Throat: Move to a quieter place. Get a different job. Love yourself. Practice acceptance and gratitude. Stop blaming.

Cecilia from Argentina has a dialogue with her hips. She says, "I have a lot of trouble with my hips and legs. They are too big to my taste, so I am always complaining about them. I use long skirts so that no one can look at them."

Cecilia: Hello fat hips, tell me about yourself.
Hips: When I am alone I am OK, but when I have to dress to go out I feel fat.
Cecilia: What is your purpose for being in my life at this time?
Hips: I am here to tell you that you have a belief in your head that says something is always wrong and that you cannot be 100 percent OK.
Cecilia: What can I do to help you feel really good?
Hips: Know that you are worthy and lovable exactly as you are. Know that you deserve to feel good in your body. Know that you are beautiful.

Great art is in exquisite balance. It is restorative. I believe in the energy of art, and through the use of that energy, the artist's ability to transform his or her life and, by example, the lives of others. I believe that through art, and through the projection of transcendent imagery, we can mend and heal the planet.

• • • Audrey Flack

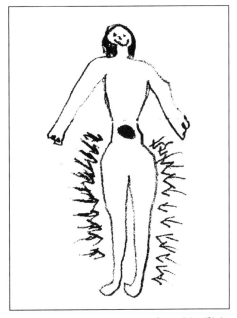

Body wisdom focus on hips (Cecilia), crayon, 1997

EXERCISE:
Dialogue with Your Body

1. Find a place to sit quietly for about twenty minutes without disturbance. Breathe for one minute, becoming consciously aware of your body. Imagine a golden ball of warm, loving, healing light above your head. Imagine that without any effort on your

The mechanism of the imagination is still a scientific mystery.

• • • Sir Herbert Read, *Child Art*

I had an upper-respiratory virus four years ago that affected my sense of balance. My first picture (me without power) was a jagged outline of my body. My second picture (me in my power) was a solid outline of my body. This tells me I need to maintain my own center first and only later listen to others.

• • • Sonja from Australia

part, this ball of light descends down into your head allowing you to look around inside. Are there sensations in your head? Continue down through the neck, shoulders, chest, stomach, intestines, organs of reproduction and elimination, and legs, all the way to your toes. Notice sensations (pain, tingling, tightness, warmth, coolness).

2. Using crayons, pastels, pencil, or pen, and your nondominant hand, draw a simple outline of your body and color in the areas where you felt sensations. For example, a tightness in the shoulders could be depicted by heavy black lines or pain by red jagged marks. Tingling in the hands could be yellow lines, pains in the heart could be red spirals, and so on.

3. Choose one sensation, one area of the body to explore with a written dialogue. Write the name of this body part on your paper: stomach, head, knees, heart.

4. Write with the dominant hand: Tell me about yourself. Sit back again and get quiet. Close your eyes if necessary. Don't analyze it — feel the sensation. Write what your body tells you with your nondominant hand. Let the sensation speak. At first it may seem silly or empty or bad or sad. Your task is to accept it. Later on you can determine if it has merits. For now, open your heart and allow your body to speak.

5. Now write with the dominant hand: What can I do to help you feel really good? Sit back again and get quiet. Don't try to figure it out. Feel the sensation again. Write the answer with your nondominant hand.

6. Ask any other questions that come to you. Answer with your nondominant hand.

7. When you finish, put the drawing a little distance away from you and look at it. Notice your feelings and your thoughts. It is not yet time to judge or determine the merit of the drawing. Write in your journal. Thank your body for sharing with you. Thank yourself for listening! Next week you can determine the merit of your drawing.

art is love

This very simple drawing exercise is always an eye-opener for adults who have no idea of the benefits that drawing can bestow on them. Whether one person does this alone in a small room or a group with fifty others in a hotel ballroom, powerful insights flow from focusing on these few steps. I begin many of my classes and workshops with this exercise. People are initially comforted and completely surprised by their own inner wisdom.

L is for listening to life with love. When you listen with love you hear the subtle side of life. We all hear the radio, the teacher, or the baby in the next room. When you listen with love you hear much more. For example, you may hear emotion in the teacher's voice (fear, excitement, hesitation). A mother can tell whether her baby is hungry, angry, or scared. When you listen to the still, small voice in your own heart, you sense different things. Sometimes you hear a voice, sometimes you feel a pressure, tingle, ache, or pain. Sometimes

Art is love, ink, 2000

you have a dream or get an idea. This drawing exercise helps you tune in to the subtle wavelength of your heart and to gain access to its important inner wisdom.

O is for opening to life with love. Most of us have an agenda or a list of things we need to do. It is important to have goals, lists, plans. Yet sometimes those things can become too important, blocking us from seeing what is right in front of us. When we consciously open our hearts to life with love, we feel safe to connect with the world around us and within us.

V is for valuing life with love. When you value something, be it a beautiful vase, a rosebush, a home, a child, a spouse, even a pair of shoes, you take care of it. All the drawing exercises will guide you to lovingly value life in its many forms. It is easy to value something that you can see, touch, or taste, but what about the things that are formless, like dreams, feelings, hunches, ideas, or intuitive insights? How do you value the still, small voice inside your heart? You listen and open your heart. Then you follow your heart. Following your heart is the same as taking action. It is a powerful signal to the universe that you really mean business.

E is for expressing life with love. It is totally natural to express life with love, once you have listened to and valued what your heart has told you. There are no tricks, no techniques, no gimmicks needed. By listening, opening, valuing, and expressing, you enrich all areas of your life.

EXERCISE: Art Is Love

1. Sit, breathe, and relax your tummy, wrist, and jaw.
2. Use your nondominant hand. With crayon, pen, or pencil, draw a vertical line down the middle of your paper.
3. Focus on an issue that concerns you.
4. Write "Up until Now" on the upper left side of the paper and below make marks or draw a picture that expresses how you have come to feel about this issue. Scribble, slash, swirl, plod, move carefully, make a mess, be precise. Allow your heart to guide your hand. When you feel you have satisfactorily expressed this issue, move on to step 5.
5. Write "What Love Would Do Here" on the upper right side of the paper.
6. Sit, breathe, relax, and drop your awareness into your heart for a moment. Look for a little door at the very back of your heart. This door opens out into the infinite part of you where unconditional love dwells. Feel unconditional love flowing into your heart and into this issue that is concerning you.
7. When you feel ready, let the love draw a picture or make marks on the right side of the paper. Love speaks like a child. Just be open and willing to allow this love to take form.
8. When you feel complete, give your drawing a title or name. The gift of love is often a whole new way of looking at an old issue. A simple shift in thinking can transform your life.

Art is love exercise (Kathy), graphite, 2000

Woman fearing the worst, ink, 2000

releasing fear

Fear is said to be the greatest enemy of the human race. It operates silently and unconsciously, preventing people from talking to one another, working together, and taking action to correct problems. Problems always prevail when fear is prominent. And problems always loosen their grip when love and dialogue get the upper hand.

Every person who works to release some of his or her fear is doing the world a great service. Love gives you strength to face your fears. When you run away from your fear, what happens? The fear grows bigger. When you look directly at your fear what happens? The fear becomes smaller and can even disappear.

Look at your fear and see for yourself that the powerful truth behind fear is love. This exercise will help you get beyond the fear to go for the love. As you can see from the list below, you could choose from plenty of fears:

Fear of change
Fear of the unknown
Fear of the dark
Fear of light
Fear of poverty
Fear of wealth
Fear of dying
Fear of living fully
Fear of falling
Fear of a mistake
Fear of dogs
Fear of flying

Fear of accidents
Fear of speaking
Fear of rejection
Fear of failure
Fear of success
Fear of weight
Fear of illness
Fear of punishment
Fear of rejection
Fear of abandonment
Fear of being alone
Fear of crowds
Fear of disapproval
Fear of differences
Fear of beginnings
Fear of endings
Fear of computers
Fear of loss
Fear of test results
Fear of being wrong
Fear of violence
Fear of disease
Fear of government
Fear of war

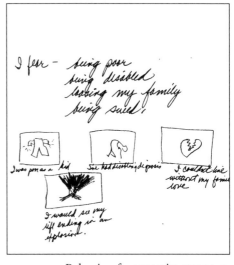

Releasing fear exercise steps 1–3
(Sue), ink, 2000

EXERCISE: Releasing Fear

Part One: Naming the Fear

1. Use your nondominant hand. In crayon, pen, or pencil, write, "I fear" at the top of your paper. Finish that sentence in four different ways.

2. Draw a box for each fear and make marks in it that express how you feel about that fear.

3. Write briefly about why you have that fear.

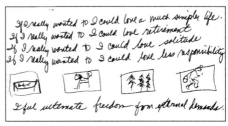

Releasing fear exercise steps 4–6
(Sue), ink, 2000

147

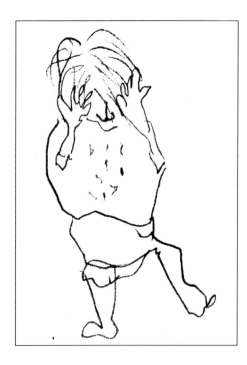

I Approve of You
I love your
bright smile
You are doing
the best you can
I love you

Letting go of shame exercise (Tory),
ink, 2000

Part Two: Shift from Fear to Love

4. Rewrite your list of fears. This time write: "If I really wanted to I could love," and finish the sentence for each fear. By choosing to focus on the love rather than the fear, you build a new pathway in consciousness. Every time that fear comes up — and it will — feel the love.
5. Draw a new box for each loving statement and fill it with marks that express this love.
6. Write a simple statement that expresses how this new pathway of love feels to you.

letting go of shame

Children are shameless. They run naked, delight in yelling and screaming and skipping and jumping anywhere and everywhere. They holler bloody murder when they are hurt or angry. Adults, on the other hand, have learned to mind their manners when out in public, to be quiet, to be clothed, to be nice.

It is important that children respect others and learn the ways of society without being made to feel ashamed of themselves as they learn. Judge the child's behavior — not the child. Correct the child's behavior, and praise the child's ability to learn.

Many adults were judged as children. They have grown up to be nice people on the outside while feeling explosive and not-good-enough on the inside. Many adults inwardly scold and criticize themselves just like their parents scolded them as children. You can't change the past, but you can change the old tapes.

Creativity stops when you feel ashamed. You simply cannot create when you feel in your heart that what you have to say is not good enough. If you are in a creative slump, or if you feel blocked creatively, try this exercise and open your creative valves. The child part of you can help you.

It is time to let go of feeling not–good-enough. It is time to discover your playful, creative spirit.

EXERCISE:
Letting Go of Shame

1. Sit, breathe, and relax your tummy and jaw.
2. Using crayons and your nondominant hand, draw pictures or marks that express shame and judgment. Put the shame on paper.
3. Now there is an empty space inside you.
4. Fill this empty space with words of praise. Be playful. Draw a new picture.

creative freedom

France in the late 1800s was a hotbed of artists, intellectuals, writers, and progressive-minded folks of all kinds. They gathered to discuss the nature of creativity, each speaking from her or his discipline (music, dance, painting, sculpture, science, theater, education, politics, and so forth).

There were many differences, and there was also a common ground. These individuals agreed that creativity required freedom. It could not survive in an environment of limited, dogmatic beliefs and rigid, stereotypical thinking.

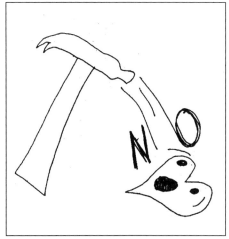

Creative freedom exercise (Cindy), ink, 2000

149

Creative freedom exercise (Cindy), ink, 2000

What exactly is a stereotype? The word was first used in the printing industry, naming the metal plate that was fixed in place and inked and pressed against paper to produce a printed newspaper, book, or pamphlet. Later, the word *stereotype* meant fixed and rigid thinking. Rigid thinking, like judgments and shame, crushes the spirit of creativity.

The French progressives yearned to live free of stereotypes, to create paintings, explore new ideas in science, economics, and law. They organized themselves as a group of free spirits and called themselves gay. Most were heterosexuals, and some were homosexuals. Thus the word *gay* to describe the homosexual lifestyle was born.

EXERCISE: Creative Freedom

1. Sit, breathe, and relax your tummy and jaw.
2. Contemplate where your spirit and creativity are crushed under rigid, dogmatic, judgmental, stereotypical thinking.
3. Draw what this feels like to you. Use crayons, and draw with your nondominant hand.
4. Contemplate where in your life you are yearning to follow your heart, to be original, to be gay.
5. Draw what this feels like to you.
6. Write a statement about what freedom feels like to you.

dissolving depression

Depression is a serious condition that millions of people struggle with. Many treatments are available, and if you are depressed, use what-ever works best for you. You can also turn to this childlike drawing exercise once a day for thirty days to explore your feelings. See for yourself the connection between depressed feelings and suppressed creativity.

Creativity is not an activity reserved for the talented few or limited to acts of procreation. It is the gift and responsibility of every living soul, says author Diana Vilas. While we preoc-cupy our minds with day-to-day details, we tend to overlook the continuous act of cre-ation. You create your own reality every day through the thoughts you think and the feel-ings you feel. What are your thoughts right now? What are you feeling right now? Can depression dissolve in creative expression just as sugar dissolves in water?

I learned that my depression is always a signal of growth. The depression signals that there is something important being suppressed. The thing to do is, if you possibly can, take a journal and some time alone. Ask the depression what it wants to tell you. It's a messenger... always.

• • • Barbara Marx Hubbard,
Crone Chronicles

EXERCISE:
Dissolving Depression

1. Sit, breathe, and relax your tummy, jaw, and wrist.
2. Focus on the depression in your body. Notice where it is. Make it okay for it to be there.
3. In crayon, draw an outline of your body. Use your nondominant hand. Draw marks to indicate the depression. Deposit as much of the depression as possible on the paper.
4. Ask the depression to tell you about itself. Ask the body part that holds the depression to tell you about itself.
5. Dialogue further if you feel there is more to say. Sometimes there will be.

Depression, ink, 2000

6. Give your drawing a title or name. If you have time, write a story about this picture.

creating money

Lack of finances often lurks in the shadows in the lives of artists and spiritual people. We want God or our creative muse or Spirit to flow through us. We work to be open to the intangible promptings of life, and we feel a bit lost when it comes to making deals, putting a price on our work, promoting ourselves, shmoozing, wheeling and dealing.

To create a good relationship with money, we don't have to shmooze, but we do have to let go of the belief that money is outside us, separate, beyond us. Money flows through you just like Spirit does. Is Spirit good but money tainted? Where do we get the idea that money is evil? Some people need to be brought to justice for their misuse of money, but that is probably not your situation.

The Principle of Abundance is eternally present like the Principle of Mother and Father. Open your mind and heart and feel its presence.

> ### EXERCISE: Creating Money

1. Sit, breathe, and relax your tummy.
2. Notice the feeling in your gut when you think of money. Using crayons and your nondominant hand, draw marks to symbolize your feelings.
3. Notice the feeling in your gut when you feel the Principle of Abundance flowing through you.

The one way in which he was proud of me was that I was not interested in money! In this one aspect of my life, he saw me as Christlike, one of the "lilies of the field." Of course, Claudia astutely pointed out, "Yes, the only way you could keep a connection to your father was to deprive yourself!"

• • • Ann Kreilkamp, *Crone Chronicles*

Woman swaying while birds fly, ink, 2001

4. Draw marks to symbolize the presence of abundance flowing through you now.

5. Name your drawing or give it a title. If you have time, have a friendly dialogue with abundance.

something's cooking!

Think about a career or vocation or project that stirs your soul — something you yearn to experience from the bottom of your heart. At this moment it may be in the ugly duckling phase. You may feel it's impossible. You may have tried a hundred times and failed every time, and now you feel like giving up. But before you give up, try this drawing exercise.

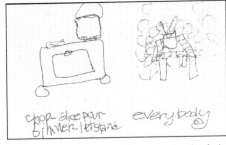

Something's cooking exercise (Babs), graphite, 2001

When Alice from New Zealand did this exercise, she saw a big spread of luscious, mouthwatering fruit. Her meal was ready to serve. She was ready to go to work. Her career needed no cooking at all. Her stove was a purple volcano. She said, "I've been focusing on spirituality lately."

Remember, some dreams and projects need to cook a bit before they are ready. We too sometimes need to cook, so to speak, to gain knowledge or experience, let go of some belief, meet someone. You carry the design for your personal fulfillment within you like the giant oak tree is carried inside an acorn.

EXERCISE:
Something's Cooking

1. Pretend that your career, vocation, or a project is food cooking in a pot, pan, or wok.

2. Describe the food: meat and potatoes, dessert, appetizer, snack, side dish, and so on.

3. Draw the stove, the pot, the food. Use your nondominant hand and pen, pencil, or crayon.

4. Describe how to best prepare and cook this food: chop, slice, pour, boil, simmer, grill, sauté, stir-fry, steam.

5. Who is coming to dinner? Family, friends, strangers — the whole world?

6. See people tasting your heart's desire and feeling fulfilled and happy.

7. Draw the dinner party.

keeping thoughts fresh

Every Sunday I purchase a bouquet of flowers from a country roadside stand near my home. They last for up to two weeks if I change the water every day. If I forget, they die in a few days. Fresh water invigorates flowers much like fresh thinking invigorates your life.

Fresh thinking is positive, loving, kind, generous, open-minded, and inclusive of others. It does not criticize or judge. It is motivated by love and takes place in the present moment, not in the past or the future. It is called thinking with the heart. This kind of thinking is a great way to cocreate a fulfilling life for yourself and other people. In ways you cannot predict, it guarantees a good life for generations to come.

Your life blossoms magnificently when you renew your thinking every day. If an important issue in your life feels stale or withered, this exercise will bring you freshness and aliveness and a new lease on life.

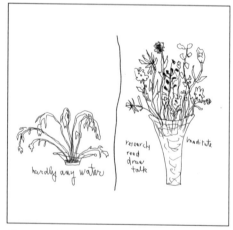

Keeping thoughts fresh exercise, ink, 2000

EXERCISE:
Keeping Thoughts Fresh

1. Sit, breathe, and relax.
2. Use your nondominant hand. In pen, pencil, or crayon, draw a line down the middle of your paper. Allow an issue that has grown stale to come to mind.
3. On the left side of the paper draw a withered bouquet of flowers to represent this issue.
4. Sit, breathe, relax, and change focus.
5. Imagine yourself swimming in an ocean of fresh, clear water.
6. On the right side of your paper draw flowers freshened with plenty of clean, clear water.
7. Give your drawing a title or name. If you have time, write a little story about the next step you will take with this issue or project.

Each of us has, within us, a unique genius. And that genius is our life purpose, our vocation. And the only way to fully mature as a human being is to identify that genius, that vocation, within yourself, and surrender to it the whole way. That is the key to the next stage of human evolution.

• • • Barbara Marx Hubburd,
Crone Chronicles

dreams and nightmares

Every new idea, new invention, new design for a chair, new painting, and new movie starts in someone's imagination. It might start as a dream, a vision, a yearning. In the beginning an idea is often a formless feeling. It may have no shape when it first comes to you as a hunch, a hope, or a sense that things could be different. Or it may come almost fully formed.

Ideas unfold through whoever is willing to work with them. Everyone gets ideas, but not everyone spends time or energy developing them. Ideas often appear in dreams. Many

Girl dreaming, ink, 2000

famous inventors, artists, and scientists claim they found the solution they were looking for in a dream.

Sometimes you wake up from a dream that really makes you wonder what's going on. You may get a book about dream interpretation or keep a dream journal. You may analyze your dream or take it to a therapist. You may forget the dream, in which case you are passing up an opportunity to discover the pearl of great price: self-knowledge.

Dialogue, rather than analysis, is my approach to exploring the ideas, dreams, and even nightmares that rise up out of the vast unconscious mind. If you are really interested in gaining information from the unconscious mind, I'm sure you will find that this approach works very well. Be the director of your own play. Provide a safe space (a piece of paper) for your dream characters to tell you what they are doing in your dream and your mind.

Dream characters can be people, cars, waves, houses, animals, rocks — anything. They are creations of your mind, so you can always ask them to tell you about themselves. When feelings, ideas, or dreams are on paper, it is much easier to develop them further, to see patterns, and to integrate them into your everyday life. Even a scary dream, when integrated, contributes something positive to your life.

Do the following exercise when you awaken from a dream or as soon afterward as you can. Parents, the following exercise works very well with children who wake up from a bad dream. Help your child find dream friends to guide them past the scary monsters. Children, by the way, do not need to use the nondominant hand, but it's a good idea for adults. Use crayon, pen, or pencil.

EXERCISE:
Dreams and Nightmares

1. Draw the characters in your dream quickly and roughly.
2. Briefly describe each character with words. (For example: Enormous woman with red apron standing in doorway blocking my path, or ocean wave coming into the house, or room full of premature babies about two inches in length.)
3. Say to each character, "Tell me about your-self."
4. Ask each character, "What are you doing in my dream?"
5. Dialogue as much as you wish. When fin-ished, give your dream a title or name.

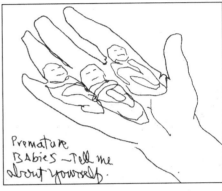

Dreams and nightmares exercise, ink, 2001

stick in the mud

Last year, a friend down the road gave us a cutting from his beautiful jacaranda tree. This is no ordinary tree. It is a beautiful purple-blossomed tree that blooms all summer.

We wandered around for a week wonder-ing where we would plant this tree that grows to forty to sixty feet high and more. We looked at the edge of our property. There was a perfect space for such a tree. We share this space with our neighbors, Bobbie and Glenn. We had been wanting to make friends with them, and this was our chance!

The deep well of our unconscious is not just the demons and devils. It's also the goddess and the ecstasy and all of our beauty. So, whenever we put a lid on the dark side, we are also putting a lid on our potential for the beautiful, the ecstatic, and the glorious.

• • • Natalie Rogers, *New Realities*

Driftwood found at Virginia Beach, ink, 2000

We arranged a tree-planting ceremony in the space between our homes. Planting this tree together seemed a perfect symbol of our new friendship. We brought buckets and shovels and had a little party.

After a few weeks, it became apparent that the cutting was not going to grow into a tree. Its leaves fell off, and it stood there naked. Nevertheless, we all continued to water it, noticing its plight and hoping it would recover from the shock of being transplanted.

All of us are busy people. Even though the tree looked like a naked stick standing in the mud, no one pulled it out. It stood there for quite a long time. Then one day, my housemate ran into the kitchen where I was standing before a sink full of dishes. With a grin, she said, "The jacaranda tree has three new leaves!"

All along it was quietly alive and growing beneath the earth's surface. It was invisible to our eyes, yet it was determined to come forth in its own time. Isn't this how life is sometimes? Careers, relationships, and projects can appear to be dead and lifeless. All of a sudden new life blossoms from the old.

I dedicate this drawing exercise to the little stick in all of us that is very much alive and well, although it ain't much to look at — right now!

EXERCISE:
Drawing a Stick in the Mud

1. Sit, breathe, and relax your tummy and jaw. Contemplate your career, relationships, finances, family life, creative expression.

2. What area of your life feels like a lifeless stick in the mud?

3. Using your nondominant hand and crayon, draw a lifeless stick. Let this stick drawing represent an area of your life that feels like it's dead, like it's going nowhere. Draw the mud and anything that you want to draw around this stick.

4. Dialogue with this stick. Ask it, "Is there life in you beneath the surface that I can't see?"

5. Answer this question. Imagine that your feelings (about a career or project) flow through your hand. Be open-hearted and childlike. Let anything come.

6. Ask further questions, such as, "Am I to be patient and go about my business and every once in a while check in on you, water you, pray over you, send love to you?" Or "Am I to awaken from the dream, pull the stick (career, project) out of the mud, and move on?"

7. Give your drawing a title or name. If you have time, write a little story and draw a picture of the tree (career or project) full grown.

navigating the world

This exercise is about work and career. It is especially about how you feel you are functioning in the work world. Work is really about service. How do you feel you are serving the world? Contemplate your job and think of it as a boat on the water. What kind of boat comes to mind? A canoe, a speed boat, an oil tanker? Are you the captain of a pleasure cruise vessel

I drew this quickly to get ready to write this book. I thought only of the woman at the helm standing confidently looking forward. That's how I feel. Yet I unconsciously drew the wind filling her sails and moving her boat backward. What is going on here? Am I going forward or backward? Well, both. At fifty-five, I am going back to college and preparing to get a teaching credential so that I can teach in public schools. I would never have consciously drawn the boat going backward, but, indeed, that is the true situation. Yet I am not upset at going backward. It is necessary that I go backward so that I can forward.

Navigating the world exercise, ink, 2000

or are you piloting a sturdy tugboat in a busy harbor? Does your craft long for the open seas? Are you in dry dock getting a leak fixed? Do you have a crew or are you alone? What powers your boat: wind, waves, a small engine, a big turbo engine? Or are you pulling the boat by hand with ropes?

Then there are the forces you need to be aware of when you navigate the world: storms, tidal movements, submerged icebergs, kelp fields waiting to curl around your rudder.

Our work self is one of the images we use to navigate in the world, says Pat Allen, author of *Art Is a Way of Knowing*. She describes a particularly rough phase she went through when she was changing careers. She saw herself clinging to rotted pilings, the boat having broken up and washed away. Despite being scared, she let go and let the river carry her along. It was an exhilarating experience of renewal for her. Eventually she washed up on a sunny beach and began building a new boat by reinventing her professional self.

A woman in one of my classes saw herself valiantly swimming with a rope around her waist, pulling a beautiful and very large yacht. She realized she was working way too hard — she had fallen into a routine of working really hard and feeling small — because she had forgotten her true capacities. This realization startled her. She got out of the water, climbed onto the yacht, stood in the captain's station, started the engines, and got back on track with her career.

Long ago people lived their whole lives doing just one job, working at one company, farming, defending the castle, or watching the herd of cattle, sheep, horses. Today, at least in the United States, most people have several careers, and many middle-aged people are back in college getting credentialed in a whole new line of work.

For this reason, you can see that for many work has become a fluid medium, changeable, highly sensitive and responsive to the ups and downs of the stock market, global trade issues, political shifts of power, energy and technological issues, to name just a few of the influences that affect our jobs.

Flexibility and a willingness to change are positive attributes in today's work world. Knowing your true identity as consciousness helps also. You are the ability to think, so use this ability to think of yourself as capable in all your adventures.

Navigating the world exercise (Cindy), ink, 2001

EXERCISE:
Navigating the World

1. Sit, breathe, relax. Contemplate your job and get clear on how you feel about your work.
2. With your nondominant hand, draw a simple picture in crayon, pen, or pencil of your boat in the water. There are plenty of choices: sailboats, rowboats, cruise ships, yachts, canoes, kayaks, heavy industrial cargo boats, pleasure boats, racing boats. Notice what shape your boat is in. Is it a brand-new boat, a restored classic beauty, an odd antique? Is it in need of repair?
3. Draw yourself in the picture on the boat

and anyone else that you want to be in this picture.

4. What kind of day is it today? Stormy or clear?

5. Draw the environment. Are you tied to the pier? In dry dock? Ready to set sail? Tossing like a cork in high stormy seas?

6. Give the boat a name. If you have time, write a story about the boat's adventures.

consulting the elder crone/old wise man

This little exercise has been so helpful to me at various turning points in my life that I just had to include it. If you are at a turning point, and you are asking big questions about whether you should do this or that, this drawing exercise is for you.

Wisdom is not gender based; however, our approach to wisdom is often colored and influenced by our conditioning. If you are a woman, consult the elder crone. If you are a man, consult the old wise man. I see no reason why you cannot cross the line, if you would like, and consult either one.

This drawing exercise takes you to a place inside yourself where you can see your present situation in relation to the full length of your life. The answer that you receive is a clear feeling of "yes — do it!" Or "No, this is not the path for you to take at this time." Mentally project yourself forward in time to the last few moments before you leave this earth. See yourself, now an elder crone or wise old man, lying on your

The crone is bridging the two worlds. She is looking at the finiteness of her life and feeling her connection to spirit. She is getting closer to the end of her life — she sees the doorway. Because she has experienced more of life, she has more perspective, a closer connection with spirit.

• • • Laura Lacy, *Crone Chronicles*

The last moment, ink, 2000

deathbed. Ask the dying crone or the old wise man to give you guidance. How does the elder crone or the old wise man feel about the decision you are making today? So many people are afraid to take a risk, to turn a corner, to take a class or a different route home. As they age, their lives become smaller and smaller. By old age they regret that they didn't stop to smell the roses more often. Don't let this happen to you.

When I was about nine years old, *Life* magazine published an entire issue about the future. Artists drew pictures of people clothed in brightly colored climate-controlled, skintight fashions, and everyone shaved their heads. To me, it was a free, uncomplicated, and cool image.

When I was forty-six years old, I decided to shave my head. I always wanted to do it but I wondered if it was a really stupid thing for me to do. My sister was concerned for me. I was a self-employed artist and teacher. Would I lose my clients? Would my students run away? I consulted my inner child and my elder crone. Both were delighted with the idea. So I shaved my head. My mother cried in horror, of course; however, in the year that I had a shaved head, no one ran away and I lost no work. Life went on while I played with this symbolic act of self-discovery and self-empowerment.

You can always consult the elder crone or the old wise man, because these figures are aspects of yourself. When you are facing a tough situation (be it spunky and fun or serious and full of consequences) do this exercise. After you access the wisdom inside you, you may also wish to consult with various professionals and see what they have to say.

Creating is an act of self-determination and self-discovery. Whether connecting brush to canvas, pen to paper, or bow to string, the creative gesture represents a decision to expose myself to mystery and uncertainty. To reveal. To intend. To dream. To see. To be. I have come to my creative life kicking and screaming, demanding to be heard, yet rarely listening. Learning to follow my inner calling has been a slow deliberate process, and a liberating one.

••• Sandra Garbrecht, *Crone Chronicles*

A crone, ink, 2000

<table>
EXERCISE: Consulting the
Elder Crone/Wise Old Man
</table>

EXERCISE: Consulting the Elder Crone/Wise Old Man

1. Sit, breathe, and relax.
2. Imagine leaning toward the elder crone or the wise old man, who lies on her or his deathbed. Whisper to her or him about your situation. (I am considering getting married, going back to school, moving to China, adopting a child.)
3. Ask, "Is this the right thing for me to do? Do I move forward with this?"
4. Notice your feelings; a lighthearted feeling spreading all over you tells you, "Yes! Do it!" A sad or sinking feeling tells you, "No! You must not do it."
5. With your other hand and in crayon, draw marks or write words cementing this experience in your consciousness.
6. Thank the elder crone for sharing her wisdom. Thank the wise old man for sharing his wisdom.

ink and intuition

exploring your intuitive feelings

My mother the mermaid, ink, 1999

Learn to live back and forth between matter space and mind space.

• • • Thane Walker, from my class notes

INTRODUCTION

the journey of unfolding consciousness

All forecasts for the years ahead point to a period of unprecedented rate of change. To cope with the pressures and to seize opportunities such a period will present we need to become more creatively flexible and imaginative. Thus, the most important ingredient for facing the future confidently may well turn out to be creativity. (Eugene Raudseppa and G. Hough, Jr.)

Life is a journey, an unfolding of a greater understanding of what life really is. To unfold something is to gradually peel back the outermost layers to reveal what it is inside, below the surface. It is good to know that deep inside you is a special place that cannot be hurt, broken, or damaged in any way. This essential part of you is timeless, spaceless, and dimensionless, and it is available any time of the day or night. Problems can be solved and bad experiences can be transformed simply by opening your mind and heart and letting a greater understanding unfold in your own conscious awareness.

The grave is not the goal of life. Greater understanding is. Every experience in your life offers you the opportunity to open up and experience this greater understanding.

A closed mind and heart stand opposed to greater understanding. Your point of view can be frozen in fear, locked in beliefs of lack and limitation, bound up in expectations. But these are only beliefs — and beliefs can be changed.

There are moments in our lives when we seem to see beyond the usual. Such are the moments of our greatest happiness and our greatest wisdom. If we could but recall this vision by some sort of sign. It was in this hope that the arts were invented . . . sign posts on the way to what may be . . . sign posts toward a greater knowledge.

• • • Robert Henri, *The Art of Seeing*

Woman on a journey with her staff, ink, 2000

You simply cannot see clearly if you are controlled by preconceptions.

• • • James L. Adams

Beliefs, memories, emotions, dreams, prejudices: all affect your point of view, but they are not you. Your age, height, weight, education, and all the various roles you play affect your point of view, but they are not you. When you awaken from a dream, you know your dream is not who you are. It is easy to see that you are far more than your physical body; just look at how different your body is today from how it was when you were a little baby! Something inside you does not change through the years, even though the outer part of you does alter with time.

You are a multifaceted human being playing many roles in life and experiencing many changes from birth to death. Through it all you are the ability to think and govern thought. You are awareness, consciousness — the ability to have a point of view. As consciousness you can change your point of view or not change it. Changing your point of view makes everything new. Life looks very different when you open your mind and heart to a greater understanding, regardless where you focus your attention.

In this book you are working with your perception, and you are learning that your perception can be focused outward on the exterior world of people, places, and things. It can also be focused inward so that you can become more aware of your emotions, dreams, and bodily sensations. You are also discovering that you may choose to center yourself and explore a deeper part of the world within you — your intuitive feelings.

At the end of the corridor of reason, where the mind draws a blank, stands a hidden doorway into the imagination. It is through the imagination, the realm of pure possibility, that we freely make ourselves to be who or what we are.

• • • Jan Valentin Saether

Randall sleeping, graphite, 1984

Blank as a piece of uncarved wood yet receptive as a hollow in the hills.

• • • Lao-tsu

Life is a journey, and creativity is a big part of it. Creativity makes the journey exciting, uplifting, and personally meaningful. The greatest gift of creativity is that it opens your heart, offers you choices, and enables you to author your own life.

Be not afraid to let go of your petty reality in order to grasp at a great shadow.

• • • Antoine de Saint-Exupéry,
The Little Prince

intuitive feelings are seldom logical

An intuitive feeling is a knowing that comes from deep in the center of your being. It may not be logical. It may have no visible connection with a memory of the past or with the physical place where you stand in the present. It may seem like a strange idea, an unlikely hunch, an out-of-the-blue thought. It feels important, but since you do not know why it should be important, you argue with it.

Usually it is a little thing. I remember leaving my studio one afternoon and pausing at the door for a brief moment, looking at the table. The stereo was on the table and a number of cassette tapes were strewn around it. A very quiet thought went through my mind: "Take the *Hooked on Classics* tape with you." I had no idea why I should take the tape. Logic's loud voice said, "What for?" I turned around and walked out the door. I was in a hurry to get to Sister Lucy's home. She had arranged for me to teach twelve neighborhood children a drawing lesson. When I arrived, and saw all twelve children seated around the dining room table awaiting their drawing lesson, I realized immediately that the *Hooked on Classics* tape would

Actual tree and stick man, ink, 1999

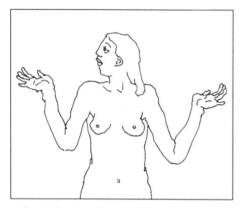

I always have a choice, ink, 2000

have been a wonderfully lively introduction to the lesson. Logic often reasons from very narrow and limited premises, and when this happens, we make logical but limited decisions.

People ignore intuitive signals feeling that these subtle messages are just not logical. While logic is a very important part of our reasoning, there are many times when logic alone is simply ineffective, even inappropriate. Logic does not motivate you to do anything. Feelings motivate you: to get up out of your chair, to take a class, to call your friend, to clean your house, to move across country.

A passionate feeling causes inventors to begin research, artists to begin creating, writers to begin writing, lovers to begin dating. If you choose a career or a marriage partner based purely on logic rather than on the feelings in your heart, chances are that you won't be very happy. Wonderful things open up in life when you allow yourself to feel deeply.

It can be frightening to feel deeply when your emotions are painful and conflicted. Say you want to become an artist, but your father wants you to become a lawyer. Or your friends want to take drugs, but you feel it is not right. What are you to do?

There are many things you can do. First, consult your heart. This book can assist you by helping you explore your feelings and your point of view. Engage the artist in you to research life issues, to solve problems, to explore the three different kinds of feelings you have (objective, emotional, and intuitive). It is the artist in you who loves to use different parts of your brain to discover new ways of looking at things.

The answers are within you. Go within and bring those answers out into the light of day. You're the only one who can do this. Blaming other people for your choices does not help you. Striking out at other people or beating yourself up is not the answer either.

You also may choose to consult a professional counselor, therapist, or minister. Join a support group. Take a class or read books to learn more about your emotions, to learn how to make decisions that are right for you, or to learn about the power of your own mind. (See the suggested reading list at the back of this book.)

Intuitive feelings are sometimes referred to as gut feelings, and they are immediate compared with intellectual logic, which is slow and has to pass through analysis. Becoming more acquainted with these three feelings (objective, emotional, and intuitive) gives you choice. Choice gives you a genuine sense of control.

change: the threshold or liminal experience

Every door has a threshold. When you stand at the threshold, you are living in between two worlds: the world outside the house and the world inside.

This is a metaphor for living during a time of change. We are living in a time of global change today. We are living on the threshold between an old worldview and a

Liminal descends from the Latin noun, limin. It means threshold. A sensory threshold is the point at which a physiological or psychological effect begins to be produced. Liminal is related to subliminal, which means below a threshold. In addition to the barely perceptible sense, liminal now sometimes means transitional, immediate — as in the liminal zone between sleep and waking.
••• Merriam-Webster's Word of the Day, July 17, 2001

Standing on the threshold, ink, 2000

The function of a cup is emptiness. The function of a wheel cannot occur without the hole at the center. The "quick" of human relationships is liminality, and the heart of community emerges wherever the social structure is not.

••• Victor Turner, *The Ritual Process*

Among the great things which are to be found among us, the being of nothingness is the greatest.

• • • Leonardo da Vinci

Milwaukee life-drawing workshop, Prismacolor pencil, 1995

new worldview. When you live on the threshold between worlds or between worldviews, you are liminal or in between. You are no longer what you once were...and you are not yet what you will be.

When I was a child I used to go on long drives in the countryside with my grandmother where she grew up. I loved to hear her tell stories about being the youngest of thirteen children growing up on the farm in Wisconsin. In September, we saw harvested wheat standing like tepees all over the field. Grandma told us how her brothers cut the wheat and stood it to dry in those shapes. She called them shocks of wheat.

When I went to Sunday school, I read about the story of Joseph. He had a dream in which his brothers were shocks of wheat standing in a circle around him, bowing down to him. Were those shocks of wheat from thousands of years ago the same as what I saw in the Wisconsin fields in 1955? Yes. People have harvested wheat in the same way for thousands of years. However, by the time I went to college, ten years later, the wheat was no longer harvested that way. It was harvested by a machine into big round shapes. This long-standing harvesting method changed during my lifetime!

Change can shock, stun, and disorient you. Divorce, loss of a loved one or job, diagnosis of illness, a car accident, bankruptcy — even the birth of a child changes your life drastically. Smaller shocks come up daily, such as missing your flight, having your car stolen, breaking your finger, being stopped by a policeman, failing a test, accidentally backing over your suitcase, dropping a glass of milk — the list goes on.

When an entire community experiences a shock from change, it can be very challenging. Some changes — floods, hurricanes, tornados, fires, violence, infectious disease — can devastate a whole community. Luckily, we have thousands of years of history showing us that human beings do not fall apart. On the contrary, they rise to the occasion, pull together, and work with one another to face the challenges and move forward.

Today we are experiencing global change, and many of us feel a bit stressed out with the speed of all these changes. Every day the outer world bombards us with information that our inner world may not be quite prepared to handle, interpret, absorb, relate, or fully understand.

Some people fight and resist making any changes. Some get depressed and give up. Some move away hoping to avoid change in that way. Some point fingers and blame the government, the neighbors, their parents.

Is there something you can do instead of blaming and resisting change? Yes, you can work with it in a positive way. You can get in touch with your feelings. You can practice adjusting yourself to a new worldview, one that is more wholistic, more inclusive, more aligned with universal principles of timeless truth, closer to the values of your heart.

You must learn to think with the heart and feel with the mind.

• • • Thane Walker, from my class notes

Two girls looking in opposite directions, ink, 2000

The wisdom that is imparted in sacred liminality is not just an aggregation of words and sentences. It has ontological value — it refashions the very being of the person.

• • • Victor Turner, *The Ritual Process*

To be creative demands an extraordinary investigation into oneself. Talent is not creativeness. To go into it fully, and deeply, one has to go into the whole problem of consciousness.

• • • Krishnamurti, quoted in *Parabola,* Fall 2000

Sometimes we just have to adjust, ink, 2000

victor turner's threshold chart

Victor Turner is an anthropologist who studied the rituals of the Ndembu tribe in Zambia, Africa. Indigenous people around the world have employed rituals for thousands of years to mark important life passages, such as marriage, birth of a child, initiation into adulthood, initiation of the new tribal leader, and of course, death. The in-between phase of the ritual process, was especially interesting to Turner. He referred to it as the *liminal phase,* a phrase coined by Arnold van Gennep.

Turner identified three distinct phases in the ritual process: (1) preliminal, (2) liminal, and (3) reincorporation. In the preliminal phase, a shock of some kind initiates the threshold experience. It may be little or big. It may be frightening or exciting, but life is no longer the same as it was.

In the liminal phase, you are in chaos. The old world is gone, and the new world is not yet visible. For a few seconds or a few years, you feel humble, naked, vulnerable. However, all is not lost. Don't run away and hide. You can learn to endure this transitory, in-between place. It is a good time to create something new. Use the heightened energy of this very special, sacred time to refashion your consciousness and reidentify yourself with a greater understanding.

At the reincorporation phase, you return to your loved ones with a greater understanding. Your heart and mind have opened up to a profound experience. Once your mind stretches and opens up, it cannot completely close down again. In a real sense you are a new person.

VICTOR TURNER'S THRESHOLD CHART

Threshold (Liminal) Qualities	Ordinary (Ego) Qualities
Open, vulnerable	Closed at one end
Equality	Hierarchy and inequality
Totality	Partiality and separation
Nakedness	Clothing to show rank
Humility	Pride
Sacred instruction	Technical instruction
Chaos	Apparent security
Communitas	Structure
Acceptance of pain	Avoidance of pain
Absence of status	Status
Absence of property	Property
Unselfishness	Selfishness
Silence	Speech
Simplicity	Complexity
Creative order	Established order

leadership and liminality

The Ndembu, have a ritual for taking an ordinary young man from the community and elevating him into the position of tribal chief. I hope the following example ritual from the Ndembu serves as a worthy metaphor for your own elevation into a greater understanding of life. Whether you are male or female, in your unique way, you have everything that it takes to be a beneficial member of your community and a vitally important citizen of this cosmos.

Integrity, honesty, responsibility, compassion, and love all flow from the person whose [self-esteem] is high. He feels that he matters, that the world is a better place because he is here. He has faith in his own competence. He is able to ask others for help, but he believes he can make his own decisions and is his own best resource. Appreciating his own worth, he is ready to see and respect the worth of others. He radiates truth and hope. He doesn't have rules against anything he feels. He accepts all of himself.

••• Virginia Satir, *Peoplemaking*

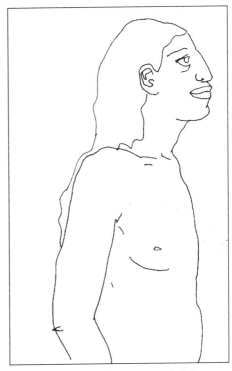

A man looking upward, ink, 2000

Ndembu Chieftainship Ritual

In the preliminal phase, the young person is removed from his home and taken about one mile away to a cage about the size of a small room. His clothing is removed. He is then locked in the cage without bedding, food, or entertainment.

During the liminal phase, the youth is naked and alone for one week. At some point members of the community come out to his cage and chide him for his selfishness, meanness, thievery, anger, and greed — all the vices representing the desire to possess for oneself what ought to be shared for the common good. Turner calls the Ndembu liminal phase of this ritual "the reviling of the Chief-Elect." Just imagine if we put our congressional candidates through this phase!

Only he will deserve the name man and can count upon anything prepared for him from above, who has already acquired corresponding data for being able to preserve intact both the wolf and the sheep confided to his care.

• • • Gurdjieff

In the reincorporation phase, the young person is removed from the cage, clothed in the chief's attire, and brought to the center of the village. He stands before the entire community, which is gathered for the celebration. An old priest makes this announcement: "Listen all you people! Kanongesha has come to be born into the chieftainship today. Look upon your friend who has succeeded to the chiefly stool, that he may be strong. He must continue to pray well to you. He must look after the children. He must care for all the people that they may be strong and that he himself should be hale. I have enthroned you, O Chief. You, O people, must give forth sounds of praise. The Chieftainship has appeared!"

Individuals in modern society often feel that the old rituals are empty of meaning.

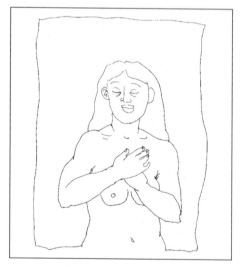

A woman holding her heart, ink, 2000

Some believe it is necessary for us to create our own rituals. Whether rituals are tribal, traditional, or new and innovative, their power to help people move through life's changes is undisputed. Drawing can be a kind of ritual. Certainly practicing the exercises in this book helps you to focus on the present and move forward into a new understanding, a new view of yourself, of others, and of life itself.

We are always standing in between the old and the new, the past and the future, the inner experience and outer experience. E. Winkler Franz, author of *Man: The Bridge Between Worlds,* says balancing these two aspects is essential for health and well-being. A person who works to balance the reality of the outer with the truth of the inner is prepared for a third reality to be born in his or her soul — the reality of unconditional love, understanding, and compassion.

In self-observation you detach yourself a little bit from the current circumstance and view the entire situation, you included, in a new light. The New England Regional Leadership Program promotes self-observation and offers the following exercise: Think of yourself as a compassionate, nonjudgmental, yet caring observer. As this observer, ask the following questions:

1. What is happening right now?
    What am I doing?
    What am I thinking?
    What am I feeling?
    How am I breathing?
2. What do I want for myself in this moment?

Confidence in your old self is lost just before you accept your new self. Instead of trying to build up confidence in the old self, be willing to plow under the partial, separate self and be planted with the seeds of your far greater Essential Self.

••• Thane Walker, from my class notes

Do I want to continue these same actions, thoughts, feelings, and breathing? Or by making myself aware of what is happening, do I change?

the value of not knowing

Sometimes my drawing students become frustrated. It is like they come to the edge of what they know and can't go any further. This is very exciting actually, because it indicates that they are ready to explore intuitive feelings, to leap into the liminal adventure of seeing their world in a new way. Liminality announces the opening of a creative space.

Instead of running back to the familiar and comfortable preliminary structures, try staying right where you are for a few moments and just observe your thoughts and feelings. Make it okay to not know, to feel vulnerable. Drawing is a safe way to practice letting go of control, to practice letting go of the need to be perfect, to practice not knowing what is going to happen next.

My experiments with intuitive drawings began in January 1999 when I sat beside my mother's bed in the intensive care unit of the hospital for three weeks. I had endless hours to draw, draw, draw. I lived as a liminal being in an altered state of mind.

I returned home to my regular routine and continued the drawing experiments for three more months. However, at home, I simply did not have endless hours to devote to drawing. In fact, I could only commit a few minutes every hour to it.

Here's what I did: Every waking hour, I

Listening to my beloved friend, ink, 2000

stopped whatever I was doing, sat still for one minute, and focused on the highest truth I know. For the next minute, I put my pen to paper and allow it to move, guided not by my conscious thoughts or by my emotional feelings, but by my gut (or intuitive) feelings. The drawings that emerge almost always surprise me. They have a style all their own. They also seem to have an uncanny relevance to whatever is going on around me or within me.

One day I was on a special assignment and had a little more time than usual to draw. After about ten minutes a woman rushed into the room where I was sitting, shouting that students at Columbine High School in Colorado were shooting one another.

I looked down at my paper and saw a child looking up into his father's eyes as the father was baptizing him. A bird flew between them. The child held the stem of a plant and seemed to be asking the father for guidance. The father seemed to be tenderly instructing the child in something sacred and loving. I felt a strangely beautiful sense of awe at the synchronicity between this drawing and the event a thousand miles away. Many fathers must have taken their children into their arms and tried to comfort, console, and teach them about life.

Father baptizing boy, ink, 1999

Intuitive feelings are a deep river running through the consciousness we all share. Connections and revelations at this deeper level are revealed to you only when you are ready to handle them. On the next few pages are two exercises to help you practice becoming friends with the intuitive feelings and gut instincts that are flowing through you.

Milwaukee trees, ink, 1996

DRAWING EXERCISES

taking a minute

People in the civilized world are always busy being productive, busy doing something. This busyness drives the economy, fills time, consumes energy, exercises the body, impresses the neighbors, and makes money. "I'm keeping busy" is a favorite expression.

Are you keeping busy, or do you make time once in a while for being quiet and doing nothing but consciously observing and being aware of what is around you and within you?

Conscious observation is not the same as judgmental observation. When we observe consciously, we are not making judgments about everyone who walks by; rather, we are viewing everything in relationship — as one connected whole. This kind of observation is impersonal, impartial, unbiased, without allegiance to any expectation or outcome. There is no need to heal, alter, fix, or change anything. We just need to be.

The one-minute exercise leaves you feeling surprisingly refreshed. In just one minute of sitting completely still not moving any muscle, you disengage slightly from your self-imposed agenda. The sounds around you suddenly register. The colors become brighter. You taste and smell what is around you. You feel the chair supporting you. This simple exercise opens a big open door to your conscious awareness. We tend to get very pointed and narrow in our scope as we rush around, meet deadlines, accomplish the task, meet the quota. It lasts only one minute — even the busiest person can find time!

It is wonderful to find something that works so well that takes so little time. Do it right now, while waiting for your child after school, or while sitting in a restaurant. If you are interrupted, just smile, and come back to the exercise later on.

EXERCISE: Taking a Minute

It is important that you be comfortable and that you feel safe to sit completely still for one minute. Move no muscle in your body — just breathe, swallow, and blink your eyes. Set your watch or clock or timer nearby.

1. Find a safe, comfortable place to sit completely still for one minute. Even in a crowded airport it is possible to sit still for one minute and not be disturbed.

2. Soften your eyes and gaze at one spot for the entire minute. Pick a spot that won't get up and walk away or move. If someone does break in, just smile, answer their need, and try again. Be kind and generous with yourself.

3. Gently unfocus your awareness. Don't think. Don't try to do this. Just be.

4. If you have another minute or two, lift your nondominant hand and reach for a pen (or pencil). Allow your slightly heightened state of consciousness to move the pen without judgment, emotion, or control on your part. Your only aim in this drawing exercise is to be open to whatever develops on your paper. Make it okay to not know what will happen on the paper. Draw for

Elementary school playground, ink, 2002

one minute or twenty minutes — whatever feels right to you. Remember, no judgments. Just be.

I dropped my attention into my heart space and found a picture of a Colorado hillside with quaking aspens fluttering in the breeze. I felt so much resonance with the aspen leaf twisting and turning by unseen forces, a flurry of frenzy and worries. Then one leaf separated from the tree and floated ever so gently to the ground — to be grounded again. I was so filled with peace and quiet and a decision percolated within me to "get grounded" more — to do the things that ground my physical body to spiritual realms.

• • • Sue from California

Feeling the light, ink, 1997

stop, drop, and feel

Some years ago I was in Los Angeles visiting a friend. My rental car was parked safely on the street outside the apartment when I retired for the night. The next morning I opened the drapes but did not see the car. It was not there! I whirled around in disbelief, anger, panic. Someone stole the car! Anxious thoughts of spending all day with the rental agency and the police and canceling appointments pursued me for at least five minutes. My blood pressure was rising as I pulled on my sweater and headed for the apartment door.

Suddenly I stopped and remembered this exercise. Stop, drop, feel. Though I felt some resistance, I stopped my chattering mind, dropped my awareness into my heart space, and felt what was there. Everything is okay, my heart said. Yes, but! I answered. I did the exercise again. Everything is okay, my heart said again. I hung onto those words, feeling the anger and panic diminish as I opened the door, walked down the hall, got into the elevator, and descended to street level. I walked around the corner and there was the car. I had not looked in the right place!

This experience taught me that I have a choice in how I use my energy. I can imagine worst-case scenarios and waste enormous amounts of energy. Or I can stop, drop, and feel. I can choose to connect with the vast source of the deep self, and save energy.

I first read about this exercise in a book by Bartholomew. Bartholomew is a most interesting character that, for lack of a better word, is a channeled being who presents clear, understandable, authentic wisdom through a woman known as Mary-Margaret Moore. Many times, I did it without drawing. It provides an immediate shift in consciousness. Occasionally, when I had the time, I drew a line. And if I had a little more time, I developed the line into a little drawing. Many of the drawings in this book come out of this exercise.

EXERCISE:
Stop, Drop, and Feel

1. Stop. Stop the chattering mind. Just stop. You can do this anywhere, no matter what is going on. If you are really in a jam, an explosive relationship, a lonely, difficult place, it is especially important to get a hold of yourself and stop your chattering mind.

2. Drop. Drop your awareness and your attention into the very center of your heart. Go to the core of your being. You know where this is. No questions. No analysis. No trial and error. Just go.

3. Feel. Feel this space. It feels a little different to everyone. It may be a little different each time you do this. But this space in you is a constant and ever-present reality. It is there for you any time of the day or night.

Man, dog, and spark, 1998

4. Draw. If you have time and a pencil, pen, or crayon, use your nondominant hand and feel your heart guiding your hand making lines, marks, maybe even an image on your paper.

Spirit doesn't live up there in the clouds — it lives in your heart. I hope you have learned to draw it into your everyday life with these simple exercises.

RECOMMENDED READING LIST

Allen, Pat B. *Art As a Way of Knowing.* Boston: Shambhala, 1995.

Arnheim, Rudolf. *Art and Visual Perception: A Psychology of the Creative Eye.* Berkeley, Calif.: University of California Press, 1974.

Cameron, Julia. *The Artist's Way.* New York: Tarcher, 2002.

Capacchione, Lucia. *The Power of Your Other Hand.* Franklin Lakes, N.J.: New Page Books, 2001.

———. *Recovery of Your Inner Child.* New York: Fireside, 1991.

———. *The Picture of Health: Healing Your Life with Art.* North Hollywood, Calif.: Newcastle Publishing Co., 1996.

———. *The Creative Journal.* North Hollywood, Calif.: Newcastle Publishing Co., 1989.

———. *Visioning: Designing the Life of Your Dreams.* New York: Tarcher, 2000.

Cornell, Judith. *Drawing the Light from Within.* Wheaton, Ill.: Quest Books, 1997.

———. *Mandala.* Wheaton, Ill.: Quest Books, 1995.

Edwards, Betty. *Drawing on the Right Side of the Brain.* New York: Tarcher, 1999.

———. *Drawing on the Artist Within.* New York: Fireside, 1987.

Field, Joanna. *On Not Being Able to Paint.* New York: Tarcher, 1983.

Franck, Frederick. *The Zen of Seeing.* New York: Random House, 1973.

Furth, Gregg M. *The Secret World of Drawing.* Boston: Sigo Press, 1989.

Goswami, Amit. *The Self-Aware Universe: How Consciousness Creates the Material World.* New York: Tarcher, 1995.

Henri, Robert. *The Art Spirit.* New York: HarperCollins, 1984.

Holmes, Ernest. *The Science of Mind.* New York: Putnam, 1988.

Kepes, Gyorgy. *The Language of Vision.* Mineola, N.Y.: Dover Publications, 1995.

London, Peter. *No More Secondhand Art: Awakening the Artist Within.* Boston: Shambhala, 1989.

McNiff, Shaun. *Art As Medicine.* Boston: Shambhala, 1992.

Nicolaides, Kimon. *The Natural Way to Draw*. Boston: Houghton Mifflin Co., 1969.

Phillips, Jan. *Marry Your Muse*. Wheaton, Ill.: Quest Books, 1997.

Rogers, Peter. *A Painter's Quest: Art As a Way of Revelation*. Santa Fe, N.M.: Bear & Co, 1988.

Saether, Jan. *The Anti-Method: Reflections on Creativity, Imagination and Myth*. Los Angeles: Bruchion Press, 1991.

Steiner, Rudolf. *Art As Spiritual Activity*. Husdon, N.Y.: Anthroposophic Press, 1998.

Turner, Victor. *The Ritual Process: Structure and Anti-Structure*. Rochester, N.Y.: Aldine De Gruyter, 1995.

Veary, Nana. *Change We Must*. Taos, N.M.: Medicine Bear Publishing, 1989.

Walker, Thane. *Philosophy of Ontology*. Culver City, Calif.: 1993.

Weschler, Lawrence. *Seeing Is Forgetting the Name of the Thing One Sees: The Life of Robert Irwin*. Berkeley, Calif.: University of California Press, 1982.

RECOMMENDED WEB SITES

Lucia Capacchione: www.luciac.com
Judith Cornell: www.mandala-universe.com
Betty Edwards: www.drawright.com
Jean Houston: www.jeanhouston.org
Barbara Marx Hubbard: www.consciousevolution.net/index.jsp
The Prosperos: www.theprosperos.org
Jan Saether: www.handtomouth.net/JVS
Heather Williams: www.drawingtogether.com

EXERCISE INDEX

PERMISSIONS ACKNOWLEDGMENTS

From *The Self-Aware Universe: How Conscoiusness Creates the Material World* by Amit Goswami, PhD., with Richard E. Reed and Maggie Goswami, © 1993. Reprinted by permission of Penguin Putnam, Inc.

From *Art Spirit* by Robert Henri, © 1923 J. B. Lippincott Company. Reprint by permission of HarperCollins Publishers, Inc.

From *Drawing on the Artist Within* by Betty Edwards, © 1987. Reprinted by permission of Simon & Schuster, Inc.

From *Man and His Symbols,* conceived and edited by Carl G. Jung and M. L. von Franz, Joseph L. Henderson, Jolande Jacobi, Aniele Jaffe; © 1969. Reprinted by permission of Doubleday NY, Anchor Books.

From *Drawing on the Right Side of the Brain* by Betty Edwards, © 1999. Reprinted by permission of Penguin Putnam, Inc.

From *On Not Being Able to Paint* by Joanna Field, © 1983. Reprinted by permission of JP Tarcher.

From *The Secret World of Drawings: Healing Through Art* by Gregg M. Furth © 1988. Reprinted by permission of Sigo Press.

From the magazine, *Science of Mind,* February 1999, Vol 72, No. 2. Excerpt by Don Miguel Ruiz.

From Rilke's *Book of Hours: Love Poems to God* by Joanna Macy, © 1997. Reprinted by permission of Penguin Putnam, Inc.

From *The Prophet* by Kahlil Gibran, © 1923 by Kahlil Gibran and renewed 1951 by Administrators C.T.A. of Kahlil Gibran Estate and Mary G. Gibran. Used by permission of Alfred A. Knopf, a division of Random House, Inc.

From *Eco-Geography* by Andreas Suchantke © 2001. Reprinted by permission of Lindisfarne Books.

From *Emotional Intelligence* by Daniel Goleman © 1995. Reprinted by permission of Doubleday Dell, Bantam Books.

From *Art As Medicine* by Shaun McNiff © 1992. Reprinted by permission of Shambhala.

From *The Search for the Beloved* by Jean Houston © 1987. Reprinted by permission of JP Tarcher.

From *Parabola* magazine, Fall 2000. Excerpts from an interview with Krishnamurti, recorded originally in Bombay, India in 1948.

From *People Making* by Virginia Satir © 2000. Reprinted by permission of Science & Behavior Books.

ACKNOWLEDGMENTS

The following people have loved me and made this book possible. I am thrilled to honor them with this book and to express my gratitude for their generous, kind, and sometimes incredibly determined hearts.

My mother and father, Edith and Ed Williams.

My life companion, Cynthia.

My sister, Gay Donahue.

Teachers: Hertha Siefert, my fourth-grade teacher; Thane Walker, Liz Andrews, Clair Gold, Billye Talmadge, and many other individuals in The Prosperos School of Ontology where I studied over twelve years; Jan Valentin Saether with whom I worked as an apprentice for five years; Louise Hay with whom I worked in a variety of capacities for over ten years.

Patricia Crane, Ph.D., with whom I worked for more than six years presenting the International Louise Hay Teacher Trainings.

Babs Smith, my workshop assistant.

Lorna Bornameier, editor-in-the-rough who helped me establish order in the chaos.

Georgia Hughes and Mimi Kusch, New World Library editors who gently and perceptively helped me clarify and expand ideas.

Mary Ann Casler, who sensitively designed the book balancing text and images for easy, indepth reading.

Tona Pearce Myers, for setting the type so that the reading flows.

Friends: Trish Kolasinsky, Analise Rigan, Merrit Hulst, Marilyn Pirkola, Mary Jo Sayer, Ned Henry, Stella Rush.

To all who contributed drawings to this book — your drawings will enable people to see how simple the drawing exercises really are and will encourage them to explore drawing for themselves. THANK YOU Cindy, Babs, Sue, Tory, Allen, and Pam of California; Kathy of Vermont, Linda of New England, Jan of New Mexico, Mary of Australia, Cecilia of Argentina, Catherine of Canada, Jeni and Karen of England.

ABOUT THE AUTHOR

Heather C. Williams teaches in the San Diego Unifed School District. She also teaches Saturday drawing classes at her studio. She has traveled and taught in England, Australia, Italy, Canada, and Mexico, as well as throughout the United States. Several hundred teachers, counselors, therapists, and healthcare practitioners in more than nineteen countries around the world use her drawing methods in their communities. Once a year she offers *Drawing As a Sacred Activity* as a seven-day intensive training program. Many of her drawings are in private collections around the United States. She graduated from the University of Wisconsin with a bachelors degree in art and humanities. She was ordained High Watch Mentor by the Prosperos School of Ontology located in Southern California. Today Ms. Williams lives with her partner, Cynthia, and their two miniature dachshunds, Twinkle Toes and Tommy, in Vista, California. For more information about her classes, workshops, and training programs, visit her web site:

www.drawingtogether.com

Heather C. Williams

New World Library is dedicated to
publishing books and audios that inspire
and challenge us to improve the quality
of our lives and our world.
Our books and cassettes are available
at bookstores everywhere.
For a complete catalog, contact:

New World Library
14 Pamaron Way
Novato, California 94949
Phone: (415) 884-2100
Fax: (415) 884-2199
Or call toll free: (800) 972-6657
Catalog requests: Ext. 50
Ordering: Ext. 52
E-mail: escort@nwlib.com
newworldlibrary.com